Valentine's Day
Cut & Paste
WORKBOOK FOR PRESCHOOL

Plus Coloring! Ages 3+

Fill the heart box with candies!

Paste the hea

Copyright 2022 Busy Kid Press. All rights reserved.

Fill the heart box with candies!

Paste the hot air balloons in the sky.

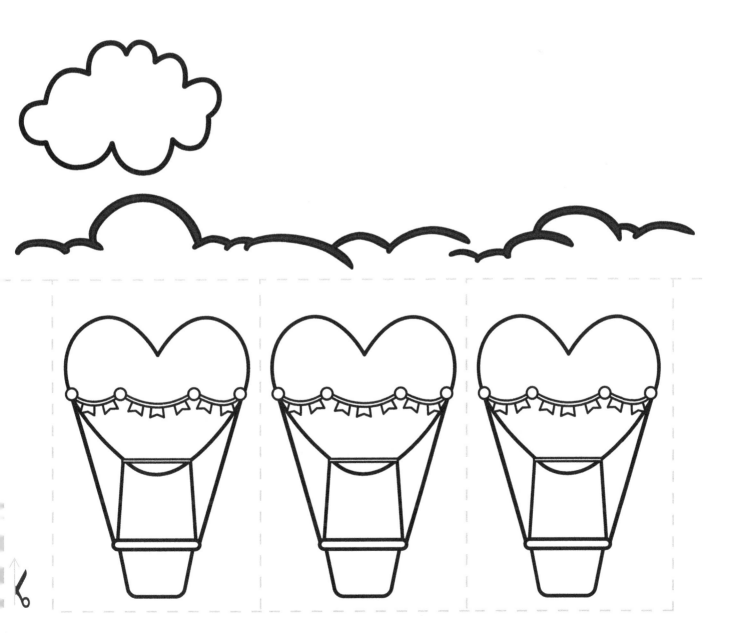

Paste the hot air balloons in the sky.

Paste the heart sprinkles on the cupcake.

What picture comes next?

What picture comes next?

Paste the heart balloons on the strings.

Paste the birds on the branches!

Paste the birds on the branches!

Fill up the basket with Valentine cards.

Paste the hearts on the flower stems.

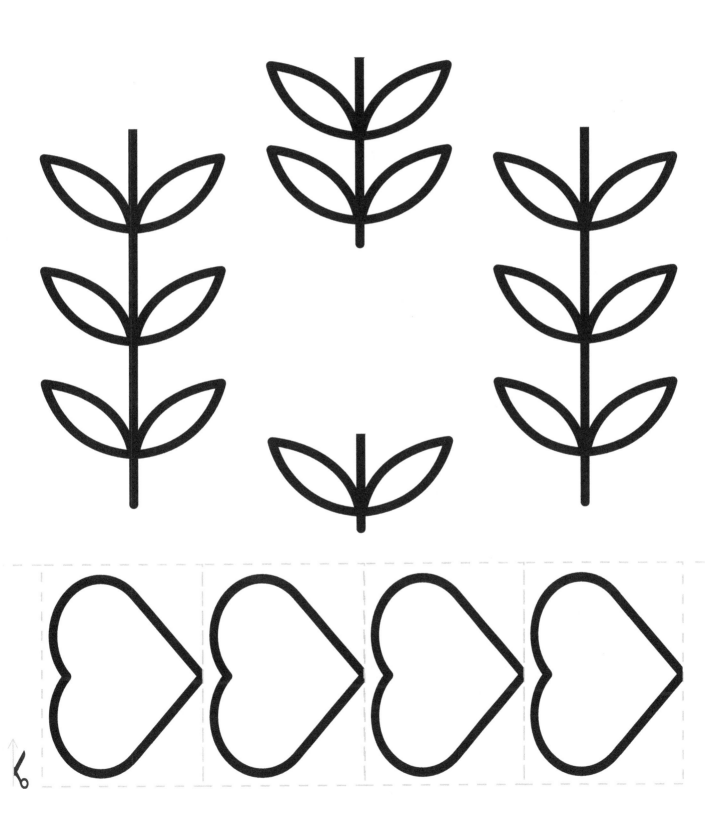

Match the pictures to the shadows.

Paste heart sunglasses on the kids.

What picture comes next?

Balance the balls on the seal's nose.

Balance the ball on the seal's nose.

Match the shapes (heart, sun, star, moon)

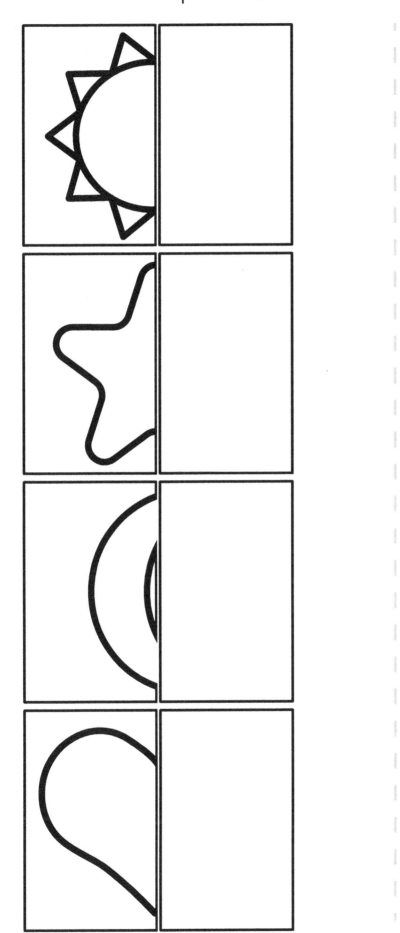
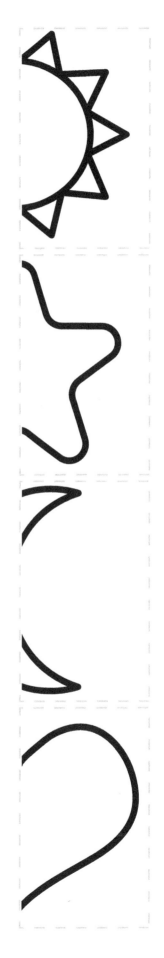

Paste the chocolates in the candy box.

Paste the chocolates in the candy box.

Paste the chocolates in the candy box.

Fill up the basket with cookies.

Paste the flowers on the stems.

Paste the animals on the farm.

How many lollipops can the elephant hold?

How many scoops of ice cream
can you paste on the cone?

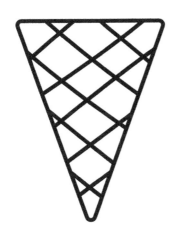

Help the boy juggle hearts.

Match the heads to the bodies!

cat   panda   unicorn

Paste sun and clouds in the sky.

Paste the arrows and feathers on the heart.

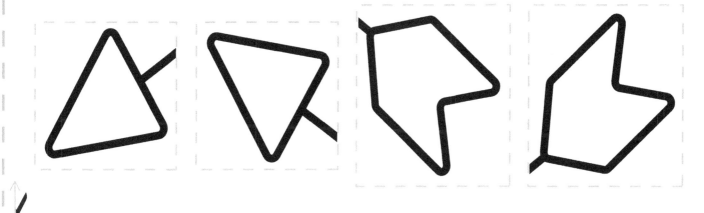

Match the pictures to the shadows.

Complete the beach puzzle!

Paste toppings on the heart-shaped pizza.

Paste the flowers on the stems.

Add the head, wings and bow to Cupid.

Stack the Valentine's Day presents.

Made in the USA
Coppell, TX
21 January 2024

27910382R00037

One thing nags at the brain a little, though. It's a question: how do those sharks get there? How are wild sharks caught? Surely it's not done the way Robert Shaw, Richard Dreyfuss, and Roy Scheider did it in *Jaws*, or there'd be no sharks here at all!

There are simpler ways than that. Walk out of the shark tank area at Sea World, back into the beautiful California sunshine, and what's the first thing you see? It's a small pool traversed by a bridge, and in the pool are many very small sharks. They're babies, and they'll grow to adulthood right there at Sea World. Attendants refer to this pool by the fond nickname, "The nursery."

The babies in this nursery may be cute, but they're also deadly. A lot smaller than the Great White in *Jaws*, nonetheless they have very sharp teeth and could very easily kill. So the question still nags a little: how do these sharks get there?

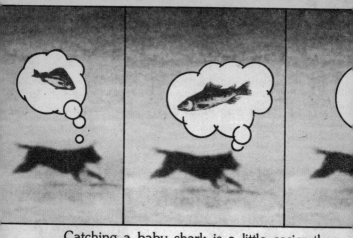

Catching a baby shark is a little easier than catching a full-grown one, but it's still not all *that* easy. Many people who live in areas with shark-infested waters nearby make a living selling baby sharks they've caught, which are then shipped to aquariums, etc., all over the world. There's even a special facility in the mid-Pacific, where captured sharks are prepared for shipment to places like— Sea World, in the United States. They're packed very carefully and sealed up tight. Most of the baby sharks are young Blacktip or Lemon sharks—generally about fifteen inches to two feet long. And once they're caught and packaged, they're off to take up residence in some faraway aquarium. But that's only *after* they're caught.

The catching process goes on all over, but one very interesting place to watch baby sharks being caught is Canton Island, which lies in the South Pacific. The island's warm and shallow lagoons draw plenty of sharks all year long. They also attract a rather amazing team of shark catchers.

THAT'S INCREDIBLE!

You wouldn't know these two are out looking for sharks. They look more like a pair of friends out for an afternoon stroll on the beach. They're not even carrying fishing rods, much less any more exotic fish-catching paraphernalia.

Nevertheless Canton Islander Tonga John and his Labrador retriever, Blackie, are out for a day's work, catching baby sharks, which is the way they make their living.

After a short period of browsing among the small waves lapping along the shore, Tonga John and Blackie go to work. Or, rather, Blackie goes to work, because Tonga John's part of the job— training Blackie to chase and catch sharks—is already done. They see a small shark, maybe two feet long, shopping for food around the shoreline.

Blackie gets going, and from the first minute it's obvious how much this dog loves his work. It's like a game of tag as Blackie chases his prey along the shore. He cuts the shark off from deeper water, keeping it in the shallows where a dog can run and

THAT'S INCREDIBLE!

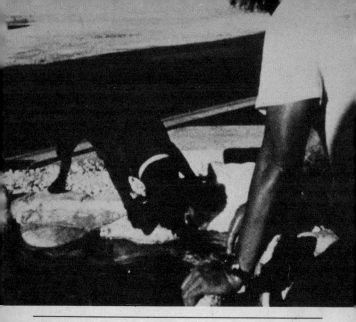

turn easily. It takes only a few minutes for Blackie to do what would take a human being hours, or even days, to accomplish. He backs the little shark into a sandy "corner," and in the instant it takes the shark to decide on a new plan of escape, the dog grabs the shark gently in his *own* jaws. Tonga John has carefully schooled Blackie in the fine art of capturing a shark without injuring it or himself.

Insofar as anyone knows, Blackie is the only shark-catching dog in the world.

And once he's caught a shark, he knows not to fuss about giving it up to Tonga John, who carefully places the newly caught prize into a holding tank.

Within minutes of placing the first shark in the tank, this extraordinary team of fishermen has

THAT'S INCREDIBLE!

found another one. Blackie gives chase, and—again, in just a few short minutes—Blackie's caught it. This time he pins the shark to the sandy bottom and then waits for Tonga John to come and help him. Cooperation obviously has a lot to do with the success of this organization!

At the end of the day each shark Blackie captures is measured and recorded. A tireless worker who loves his job, the talented dog often safely captures a dozen young sharks in a single day.

Like most contented workmen, Blackie's very proud of what he does, and at the end of the day he likes to watch over the day's catch as they swim in the holding tank. Interestingly he never bothers the sharks in the tank: once they're caught, they're caught!

Does Blackie miss the sharks when they're shipped away? Probably he doesn't. After all, there'll be plenty more sharks to catch and watch over tomorrow.

2
TOM SWIFT'S REVENGE

Here's a problem police everywhere face every day:

You're a peace officer. An armed suspect is acting erratically. You have been called to the scene to subdue him and take him in to the precinct, but he's resisting arrest. You'd prefer not to use a lethal weapon. What do you do? How do you proceed?

Put that question to Major Jack Bowlin, Director

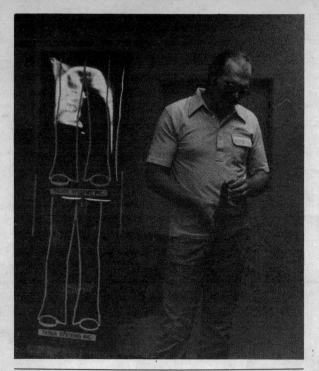

of Training at the Metropolitan Police Department in Nashville, Tennessee, and you'll get an answer that will first confuse you and then surprise you.

How does he deal with the situation just described? "Whenever you talk about the use of force, it's tough," Bowlin admits. "But there is a solution."

And what's that?

"The answer is something new called the TASER gun. We use it right here in Nashville," he says, "and we were the first police department anywhere to begin using it.

THAT'S INCREDIBLE!

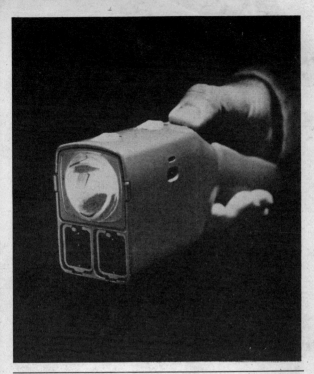

"I can recall one incident where an emotionally disturbed person became violent at home. The police were called to help subdue him, but when they arrived, he became even more violent. Police used the TASER gun, and he was apprehended without any injury or problem to himself or anyone else."

Nashville was first to adopt use of the TASER gun (which, like any other gun, requires a gun license for its owner), and eventually more began to use it, so that now a total of thirty police departments nationwide are making use of the TASER.

Still confused about how one gun can be better than another? Well, this gun is like no other weapon you've ever seen. It looks like a Buck Rogers cosmic ray gun. But it was invented right here in the United States by a man named John Cover.

John Cover explains how the gun works and why it's so much safer than a conventional gun. The reason is that the TASER doesn't shoot bullets. It shoots *electricity* instead.

"Our bodies are essentially electrical," Cover explains, gently turning his invention in his hand. "Everything that we think and do is organized by electrical currents. The TASER projects two contact units that inject electrical current into the body, and those two units overpower your own natural system. The shot from this gun causes your muscles to contract involuntarily, and when that happens, you lose your balance and fall, stunned."

Viewers of *Star Trek* are probably thinking of the number of times Captain Kirk directed his crewmen to set their phasers on "stun," since those guns affect their targets in much the same way. Did Cover name his gun the TASER as a way of mimicking *Star Trek*'s phaser?

Cover winces a little at that question, perhaps wishing he'd come by the name that easily. "I was afraid that question would come up," he says with a laugh, and then explains the *real* origin of the name. "A number of years ago there was a fictional inventor named Tom Swift. He had a noiseless airplane, a wonderful motorcycle, and he also had an electrical rifle.

"I read about that electric rifle when I was a kid,

THAT'S INCREDIBLE!

and years later I had the opportunity to become an inventor myself. What I created was this particular gun, so I felt I had to call it *Tom Swift's Electric Rifle.*

"Of course," he adds quickly, "we had to make it Thomas *A.* Swift, so that people could pronounce it."

However it got its name, the TASER gun is a fabulous invention that has already saved many lives and is destined to save many more.

Ask to see a demonstration of the gun at work, and a few problems arise. To see it in action truly requires a human being. But a preliminary demonstration can be made with the help of a special target.

The target is designed to show the effects of electricity. A plastic sheet with aluminum coating covers the front, and it will conduct the high-voltage electricity, except where the aluminum has been removed.

First, Cover has to load the TASER gun. The round of ammunition is contained in a cassette which snaps onto the body of the gun. With the cassette in place, the inventor aims at the special

THAT'S INCREDIBLE!

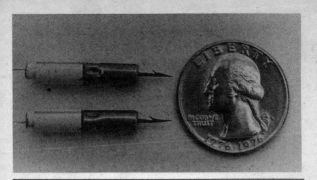

target and fires. When Cover fires at the target with the TASER gun, the two contacters are clearly visible as they hit the target, and then stick to it.

"You can probably see the high-voltage sparks," he says. In addition there are impressive, very visible tentacles of electricity. It's quite a sight.

A button on the gun controls how much voltage is used. And the person who is firing the gun can also decide how long to continue the voltage after the target is hit.

Watching the TASER work on a special target is interesting, but watching it work on a genuine human being would be incredible. On one occasion when the amazing new gun was being demonstrated, someone actually volunteered to allow himself to be hit by the gun.

The man's name was Roger Kyle. Crazy or not, he willingly allowed himself to be used as a practice target. Why in the world would someone submit to such a thing, if he didn't absolutely have to?

"Well, I believe in the TASER gun," said Kyle confidently. "I hope it will prevent some deaths in police work." There's nothing like putting your beliefs on the line! And volunteering to stand still and

allow someone to shoot fifty thousand volts of electricity through you is some way to do it. . . .

Still Roger was willing and ready, but admittedly afraid. "Most definitely," he said.

As soon as Jack was ready, Roger braced himself for the coming electrical barrage. Whether or not he had any idea what he'd let himself in for, no one could truly say.

Jack raised the TASER gun, took careful aim, and fired.

In a split second Roger Kyle was hit. He arched his back, lurched slightly, trembled violently, and fell to the floor. Presumably, had Roger been a criminal or other violent person, police would have waited for him to fall, then taken the opportunity to run to the stunned body and handcuff their suspect. But on this occasion John Cover ran to the stunned "target" and removed the two tiny contact projectiles.

Soon after falling to the ground, Kyle was struggling to sit up, rubbing his forehead, shaking his

THAT'S INCREDIBLE!

head back and forth as if trying to clear it of fog.

"Are you all right?" someone asked.

"A little nervous," he said woozily, but he was obviously all right.

Later he described the sensation of being hit by the TASER projectiles. "When they first went into me, the darts didn't feel too comfortable." So there evidently is considerable pain involved—but better a little brief pain than a gunshot wound or even the possibility of being shot dead. Very soon after the TASER shot, Kyle was almost back to normal, with an extraordinary memory of the event behind him but no permanent aftereffects.

The reaction exhibited by Roger Kyle was familiar to Major Bowlin of the Nashville Police Department.

"The reactions we've witnessed are virtually the same," says Bowlin. "We seize the moment when the person is stunned to apprehend. That is certainly a better solution than lethal force."

Roger Kyle exhibited no aftereffects, and inventor John Cover concurs that there aren't any. "It's been thoroughly, medically proven," he says, with obvious pride. "I'm happy to say that, in hundreds of uses, no one has been seriously hurt."

As Roger Kyle, who believes in the future of the TASER gun, so bravely showed by allowing himself to be shot with it, there is definitely a safer and more humane alternative to the use of firearms. According to Major Bowlin, thirty police departments across the nation have adopted the use of John Cover's ingenious, life-saving device.

Let's hope that in the foreseeable future, those innovative law enforcement groups will be joined by many, many more.

THAT'S INCREDIBLE!

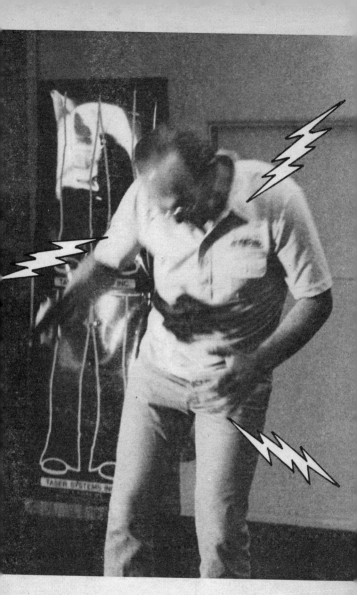

3
BUNGEE JUMPERS

Do you ever tell yourself that the sport you love best, the one you've been playing all your life, is kind of dangerous? Is that tiny—or even large—measure of sheer peril one of the things that makes the sport appeal to you? Maybe you enjoy the fact that people are always warning you to give up rugby football, no matter how much you love that bumper sticker that reads "Give blood: play rugby." Perhaps the thrill of going sixty-five miles an hour in a ski race (as well as the thought of what might happen if you zigged when it would have been better to zag) is knowing you're really laughing in the face of death.

Well, what would you say if someone told you that those were sissy sports compared to some you might take up? Would you call the speaker an envious nut? Don't do it, because if ever someone says that to you, it would be nice to know in advance that he's right.

Somewhere in the world, right now as you're reading this, there's a group of daredevils who come right out and call themselves the Dangerous Sport Club. And they're not kidding. They travel the world in search of unbelievably dangerous feats to perform.

On March 6, 1980, they gathered in Colorado to pit athletic skill and daring against death, depending only on long strands of bungee cord to keep them from being killed.

What, you may ask, is bungee cord?

Bungee cord is a highly elastic kind of rope, which in its smaller form is used by many people for uses such as tying books to bicycles. But there are some people who use bungee cords to support them when they jump off bridges—very *high* bridges—which is something only highly trained experts should use bungee cord for.

The members of the Dangerous Sport Club decided to jump off a very high bridge, supported by bungee cord alone, and when they decided which one they wanted, their choice was almost as extraordinary as the feat they wanted to perform. The club members chose the Royal Gorge Bridge,

THAT'S INCREDIBLE!

near Cañon City, Colorado. Eighteen feet wide and more than 1,200 long, the bridge spans a narrow, V-shaped chasm that was carved through solid granite by the relentless Arkansas River.

There's no bridge, *anywhere*, quite like it. Built in 1929, it is the highest suspension bridge in the world. It attracts visitors from all over the world because its breathtaking view of Royal Gorge is one of the most spectacular sights in America.

Before you start packing your bags, though, here's a small warning: Royal Gorge Bridge is not a place for anyone with a fear of heights. From the surface of the bridge to the river below is a distance of 1,053 feet. And the width of the rock bottom is no more than forty or fifty feet. All of which makes it a long, *long* look down!

But that's exactly the feature the Dangerous Sport Club was looking for. So on March 6 they arrived, with all their strange equipment, for an ex-

traordinary exhibition of physical skill and daring.

To look at them, the members of the club don't exactly look like an organized group of daredevils. They look more like fugitives from a mummer's parade, dressed in tuxedoes, toting bottles of champagne, and laughing as if they weren't about to risk their lives. As they arrive, a young woman is taking pictures of them.

THAT'S INCREDIBLE!

First is Jeff Tabin, a Rhodes scholar at England's Oxford University. He is in charge of the rigging and knot tying, and he goes to work on the bungee cords as soon as he arrives. Since the other members of the club try to make it a practice never to check their own rigging, Jeff—as he ties the knots—quite literally holds in his hands the lives of his friends.

David Kirke arrives at Royal Gorge Bridge wheeling in front of him a snappy-looking wheelchair, the symbol of the Dangerous Sport Club. He is wearing a tuxedo and top hat. He removes the hat, sets it on the seat of the wheelchair, then uncorks a bottle of champagne. Taking a generous swig, he says to anyone within earshot: "This is breakfast and it's bloody cold."

David is the club's leader and perhaps its most daring member. And since every jump may be his last, he insists on formal attire and a continual festive atmosphere—the reason for tuxedoes and champagne. At the age of thirty-four David is single and, like Jeff Tabin, an Oxford scholar. Occasionally David lectures in English literature at Oxford University, but he far prefers pursuing his life's three main passions—poetry, airplanes, and women, in any convenient order. This morning he's swilling champagne and laughing with his friends: for him "bungee jumping" is obviously

THAT'S INCREDIBLE!

just a casual diversion.

Alan Weston, another member of the club, is picking up his bungee rigging now that Tabin has finished checking it. He throws it over his shoulder and moves farther down the bridge to adjust its placement on the rail. Alan is a junior research fellow in aerospace engineering at Virginia Tech. In his early twenties, he regards the dangers of his hobby with studied indifference.

David Kirke is discussing the morning's business with his fellow clubbers. "... as he bounces up, he's going to tend to sway down this way, and Alan is going to be on a long rope next to him and we don't want him to bounce up and hit Alan." No one needs much convincing; the riggings are spaced farther apart.

Meanwhile Timothy Hunt is being helped into his harness. The twenty-two-year-old lives mainly in Paris and among his relations is an older brother named James Hunt, the champion race-car driver.

35

Elsewhere on the bridge is a man in a cowboy hat. He's an American studying geology in Portland, Oregon. He's testing his harness.

Looking over the side of the bridge is Anthony Murphy, an Englishman studying to be a lawyer. His wife, Sophia, is also a member of the club. If Sophia's worried about what her husband is preparing to do, she doesn't show it. Soon they're even joking about the jump.

"After months of training," Anthony says dryly, "I now know how to let go of a bridge." He wags a cautioning finger at his wife. "Just don't push."

As if on cue, she gives him a little shove as she says, "I'm not."

The jumpers may take the subject of their safety lightly, but others have taken precautions to safeguard it. *That's Incredible*'s field producer, Seth Hill, has coordinated a method of transporting the jumpers in case of injury, and as preparations get under way, he discusses his plans with the medics and assistants he's brought with him.

"If we've got an injury," says Seth, "if there's a man injured and he's not dead yet, we have to get him out real fast. We may have to fly up and pull the gear out of the chopper. How long does that take?"

"About three minutes," comes the answer.

"Three minutes," Seth echoes. "Well, we could take one of you medics down there, get the man on the chopper, bring him to the ambulance or else fly him to the nearest hospital, whichever is quicker." He pauses to think a minute. "Let's assume he's got broken ribs and a broken leg. If they have to haul him up on the cable it could be fifteen minutes. What would survival time be in severe

THAT'S INCREDIBLE!

1929 ROYAL GORGE 1979
SUSPENSION BRIDGE
"HIGHEST IN THE WORLD"
Construction begun May.1929 • Dedicated & opened Dec.8,1929
3,397 VISITORS TO   572,877 VISITORS TO
ROYAL GORGE in 1929   ROYAL GORGE in 1978
HANGING BRIDGE CONSTRUCTED 1878-79   FIRST TRAIN IN ROYAL GORGE-RAIL,1879
LAST PASSENGER TRAIN IN ROYAL GORGE-JULY, 1967

THAT'S INCREDIBLE!

shock? Do you know?"

A medic responds, "Until he goes into cardiac respiratory arrest—as long as his heart and lungs are working—he's got time. If he goes into arrest, we've got about four minutes."

This conversation is going on within easy hearing distance of the soon-to-be-jumping bungee jumpers, but if the grim possibilities being discussed bother them, there is no indication.

The time for the jump is now drawing near. On the bridge, a thousand feet above the Arkansas River, the final preparations begin. This is the time when throats get dry and stomachs begin to quiver just a little. The champagne helps.

David Kirke is being strapped into his harness. "Very good for the old waistline, this sport," he says, grinning. Alan Weston is tying his tie; Timothy Hunt is adjusting his top hat; Anthony Murphy is popping a fresh bottle of champagne, taking a generous drink, then passing the bottle to his fellow jumpers.

Harnessed to long elastic bungee cords which are capable of stretching to double their length, the members of the Dangerous Sport Club will hurl themselves off the Royal Gorge Bridge. If the cords break, the result will be certain death.

David Kirke offers Alan Weston more champagne.

"Sure, I wouldn't mind some," says Alan, who's just been told he won't be the first to jump. "I'm really serious about jumping off, but I really can't wait too long. . ."

Is his courage fading, just a little?

"Well, if you could hold up, it would be better. It really would," David says with gentle stubborn-

THAT'S INCREDIBLE!

ness.

With some reluctance Alan finally agrees.

Two of the bungee cords, firmly attached to the bridge rails, are thrown over the side. Several strong men are stationed to hold the cord fast. The jumpers' lives will depend completely on the strength of the cord, but placement is also impor-

THAT'S INCREDIBLE!

tant: the cords are carefully positioned so that one jumper's strand will not entangle another's.

Alan Weston becomes increasingly impatient. "Can you please get to your ropes, Dave?" he asks. "Really, let's just do it now."

A small crowd has gathered on the bridge to watch the proceedings, and out in the gorge a cable car has stopped in midair to get a better view.

David Kirke obliges Alan by climbing over the bridge rail and stands clinging to the outer edge. His perch is precarious, and perhaps he realizes only now exactly how far he is about to fall.

"I'll say 'One, two, three, go!'" he tells the men holding his cord. "When I say go, you release it."

A brief silence is pierced by the sound of Alan Weston calling for another drink.

There is less than a minute to go before the jump, and Royal Gorge looks more formidable than ever before. This bungee jump is by far the greatest challenge the Dangerous Sport Club has ever taken on.

David checks out a few last-minute details, makes sure everyone else is ready, checks his own top hat, and asks someone to see to it his tails don't snag on the railing.

"Can't trust a single damn thing ...." he mutters.

Everything's just about ready now. David Kirke will be the first to jump, followed by Paul Foulon and Alan Weston. It's a tense moment, and the mood is set by yet another member of the club, Hubert Gibbs, who plays a tune on the piano they've brought along for just this purpose.

"One, two, three, go!" shouts David.

And then they're off!

The falls seems to take forever, but in fact David Kirke's is the longest. He's decided on an extra-long bungee cord that will take him almost nine hundred feet down before it takes hold and bounces him upward again.

When the cord finally relaxes and David stops bouncing at the end of his tether, he simply hangs in space—a mere hundred feet above the river.

Each of the bungee jumpers makes his fall, and

finally they're all dangling in the air, with little to do except enjoy the scenery until their colleagues pull them back up onto the safety of Royal Gorge Bridge.

The strong men on the bridge eventually begin the sweaty task of pulling each jumper back. Each jumper has escaped without injury, although Timothy Hunt's face still smarts a little from bungee-lash.

THAT'S INCREDIBLE!

Everyone but David Kirke is soon pulled back to safety. There's been a slight snag—something no one foresaw—in that the extra length of David's cord has made him too heavy to hoist by hand. Dangling a hundred feet above the river, ignorant of the problem, he waits almost two hours for something to happen. "If anybody can hear this up there," he mutters to himself, "would you tell them that it isn't very comfortable at the moment

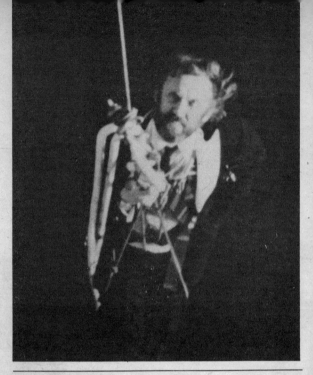

and they should really get a move on with it." Finally he's yelling, "I want to go up!"

A solution is eventually devised to handle David's problem, and after two and a half hours a tow truck is summoned to help haul David out of the gorge.

"Incredible!" is all they can say about the experience of bungee jumping in the gorge, but the Dangerous Sport Club has done it again and survived without serious injury. With matchless style and courage they've challenged and conquered Royal Gorge—their greatest feat to date.

Weeks later the clubbers have recovered from

THAT'S INCREDIBLE!

the jump and find talking a little easier.

Just how did they come up with the concept of bungee jumping from bridges?

David Kirke, as always, is quick to answer. "All we had to do was look at a bridge," he says. But, interestingly enough, bridges weren't their first choice. "We really wanted to go vine jumping in New Guinea." He explains, "They jump off these very long vines, and whoever gets nearest to the ground gets the best woman . . ." Maybe *that's* why David chose the longest bungee cord! And what would he do if the cord broke? "I might not be bungee jumping anymore, really."

Royal Gorge, of course, was not the club's first jump site. A year earlier they jumped from a bridge in England, then went on to tackle the Golden Gate Bridge in San Francisco. More jumps are planned, but the club members feel it's time for a slight change.

"We're hoping to have a parachute jump from outer space, actually," offers Alan Weston. "From 135,000 feet."

"We'd also like to hang-glide Mount Everest," says David, "but there are bureaucracy problems." There's also the small matter of special suits they'd have to wear, because of the atmosphere.

"We need a pressure suit," explains Alan. "We'd need one because at that altitude the density is so low your blood would boil. You have to protect yourself against that in some way. It's also extremely cold up there." He sounds so blasé, you'd think these were minor problems they'd easily solve.

If the Dangerous Sport Club's jump from Royal Gorge Bridge is any indication, the club members probably *will* defeat any problems that stand in their way and go on to jump from whatever strikes their fancy.

That's Incredible will be there when they do.

4
STRANGE VISITATION

The night was deep and black, a Virginia night with the crisp promise of fall. It began in September, 1975, that very night, as a woman lay sleeping. She wasn't dreaming—at least not that she knew of—but suddenly her rest was disturbed by a loud noise, a thunderous sound that made her sit bolt upright in bed.

"I could hear drums beating," said the suddenly

very awake woman later. "I was encased in earth, with grass all around me. Indians with painted faces appeared. I thought I was going to be scalped."

Then a single Indian stepped forward from the other Indians. This handsome red-skinned man was different from the rest, if only in size; he was enormous, much taller than the others.

The woman's heart began to beat wildly. She was terrified. But the huge Indian seemed to sense her fear. He raised one of his big, work-worn hands as if to stop her anxiety in its tracks. "Don't be afraid," he said. "I am your spiritual Indian guide. My name is Blackfoot, of the Crow Indian tribe."

They spoke—or rather he spoke—for moments or minutes, there is no way to say for sure. And then Blackfoot faded, as did the entire scene.

THAT'S INCREDIBLE!

The next day, struggling to recall every detail of her extraordinary experience, the woman went to a library in Virginia Beach, and there, as Blackfoot had said she would, she found a photograph of the man who had appeared to her.

But there was more. Blackfoot had described himself as being "of the Crow Indian tribe," but this was nothing if not a masterpiece of understatement. Blackfoot had in fact ruled the Crows for fifty years, until his death on a hunting trip in 1877. He had also been known by the name Sits in the Middle of the Land, Chief of all Chiefs of the Crow nation, and it was Blackfoot who had founded the Crow constitution. To the seven thousand Crow Indians still inhabiting the reservation near Billings, Montana, the memory of Blackfoot was as sacred and traditional as the memory of George Washington is to most Americans.

There was, however, a single difference. Americans have the comfort of knowing the remains of the Father of Our Country lie peacefully at Washington's beloved estate in Mount Vernon, Virginia. The Crow people had no such comfort. When Blackfoot died on that hunting trip in the Wyoming territory a hundred years ago, the whereabouts of his burial place were not recorded. No one knew where the bones of the chief were, or even how to begin looking for them.

THAT'S INCREDIBLE!

Still, on a night in September, 1975, Blackfoot presented himself to a hastily awakened woman in Virginia. Why? She had, by her own admission, never been to Wyoming—more than two thousand miles from her East Coast home—and had no particular knowledge or relation to any Indians.

As a matter of fact, quite the opposite was true: the woman's name was Victoria Mauricio, and—even if Blackfoot's choice of conversational partners seems a bit strange, it is only odd on the

surface, for Mrs. Mauricio, a woman in her early fifties, is a psychic. Who better to perceive and believe his presence? Obviously Blackfoot was encouraged by her reception and the fact that she drove to the local library to research his life: for the next two years the Chief visited her twice a week.

Finally, having heard so much about the Crow Indian people from their fallen leader, Mrs. Mauricio placed a call to the reservation near Billings. Her contact there became a switchboard operator, Clara White Hip.

"She kept calling about an Indian chief named Blackfoot," says Clara, who was eventually convinced that Victoria was sincere. It took numerous calls to convince her, but Victoria finally managed

THAT'S INCREDIBLE!

to make Clara believe that Blackfoot was in fact
appearing to her, and that he was anxious to have
his remains found and buried amongst his people
on the Crow reservation.

The result was an invitation from Clara White
Hip for Victoria Mauricio to visit the reservation. In
July, 1978—almost three years from the date of
Blackfoot's first visitation—Victoria arrived at the
site.

"I went because Blackfoot told me to get in
touch with his people. He was worried about the
lack of food there, the lack of clothes," she explains.

While she was there, she spoke to the tribal
leaders, describing to them in detail the visions she

59

had had and her encounters with Blackfoot. She told them that Blackfoot constantly said to her, "Tse-tse, Tse-tse!" which seemed to Mrs. Mauricio rather strange. She flew back to Virginia still confused, and thinking, "The 'tse-tse' is a fly in Africa, but what would that have to do with him, or me?"

Blackfoot continued to appear to her even after she had completed the task he had given her, visiting and talking with his people. Evidently he had more for her to do.

"He told me he wanted his remains returned to the Crow reservation," says Mrs. Mauricio. Then the Chief began to provide her with clues as to where his bones could be found.

She insists the clues he gave her meant nothing to her at the time. They included: a pitchfork, seven white women, a cave near three rocks one on top of the other, and a pair of trees pointing upward like fingers. But there was also the strange word "tse-tse." Could it possibly be the key that would make sense of the other clues?

The Crow tribal leaders knew that "tse-tse" probably had no great meaning, but they also knew that there is a town in Wyoming called Meeteetse. The town was in fact well known to Clara White Hip. After giving the matter much thought, the friends Victoria had made during her trip to the reservation began to believe the strange ghost story, and together they launched a search for the remains of the historical chief. Search parties were formed, and they fanned out around the Meeteetse area.

Says Clara White Hip, "During our hunt for the Chief we stopped once in a while to call Victoria and she'd give us clues to go by."

THAT'S INCREDIBLE!

David Stewart, another Bureau of Indian Affairs employee, also took part in the search. "We were guided as if by remote control," he would say later, "with Mrs. Mauricio as the controller in Virginia and we searchers in Wyoming."

The whole process amazed no one more than it did the psychic who had begun it all. "It seemed incredible to me," she says, "that during the time when the Indians were searching for Chief Blackfoot's grave in Wyoming, his spirit was here with me—directing the Indians to find his bones over 2,300 miles away!"

This round-robin method of search went on for weeks. Meeteetse and the surrounding area was combed carefully by the search parties, but no evidence of Blackfoot was found. But then Victoria told Clara of new clues she had been given: she had had a vision in which seven white women appeared, and heard a word whose meaning she couldn't imagine.

"Blackfoot was constantly saying, 'Pitchfork, pitchfork,'" Victoria told her.

"There's a Pitchfork Ranch in Meeteetse!" Clara replied. With further thought, some recalled the trees Victoria had been told of earlier, trees with upward-pointing branches—could these have been an early attempt by Blackfoot to convey the word "pitchfork"? There was no way to tell, but a search party set out right away to visit the Pitchfork Ranch. When they arrived, the searchers were astonished to learn that the heirs to the Pitchfork Ranch were seven white women. And there was more awaiting the group later.

Weeks before, Victoria Mauricio had described to the Indians a bluff with three rock figures on top.

THAT'S INCREDIBLE!

She told them the remains of Blackfoot would be found in a cave close by. In the previous weeks they had had no luck in locating the curious rock formation, but today they found it—at the Pitchfork Ranch. The date was August 26, 1978.

The party, led by Leo Plainfeather and his son Willy, set out to climb the bluff. As they neared the top, the group separated in order to cover as much ground as possible as quickly as possible. Alone, Willy Plainfeather explored the bluff's narrow caves and crevices. It was like stepping a century back in time, and after several hours Willy began to experience a powerful and eerie sensation.

"As I came close to one particular cave, I felt as if someone were pushing me closer to it," Willy recalls. "I felt like someone was pushing me toward

THAT'S INCREDIBLE!

the cave, like a force, guiding me in there, pulling me in there. I just climbed around in the cave, with the force still there, and I found the bones."

The bones were not alone. An old buffalo robe was close by, and large beads from a chief's necklace.

Richard Fletcher, a sociologist with the Eastern Virginia Medical School, later said the bones Willy Plainfeather found were very large bones, which leads anthropologists to believe that they are indeed the bones of Chief Blackfoot, a massive man who stood about six feet five inches tall. "And the extremely valuable crystal beads found with the skeleton were of a type worn only by Indian chiefs," he said.

The bones were removed from the cave, and on

October 4, 1978, the remains of a man generally believed to be Chief Blackfoot were reburied—with full tribal honors—behind the Bureau of Indian Affairs building on the Crow reservation.

The reservation's schools were let out for the event, and Victoria Mauricio led the burial procession. She wore around her neck a necklace of three translucent beads—three of those found with the bones, given to her by the grateful tribe she had befriended. Two thousand Crow Indians attended.

Today Mrs. Mauricio claims to have performed several hundred healings on the reservation, and the Crow Indians who live there have begun to refer to her as "the white Indian."

Richard Fletcher says he will be interested to see the reaction of the Crow people to Mrs. Mauricio's continued presence. "The Crows see Blackfoot as a living spirit," says Fletcher, "one who is strong enough to give Mrs. Mauricio the clues which she then related to them."

Victoria concurs completely and expands on the idea. "I was fulfilling a prophecy that had been prophesied over a hundred and fifty years ago," she explains. "It said that a great chief would be brought back by an outsider and great healing would be brought to the reservation. And it was fulfilled.

She also believes she was a natural choice for Blackfoot, coming as she does from a family of psychics and mediums. "My mother, father, uncle, and other relatives were trance mediums who could predict the future," she says. Born in Wales, Mrs. Mauricio settled in the Virginia area about fifteen years ago. "My real adviser is Rameses II," she

THAT'S INCREDIBLE!

continues, indicating that she is no stranger to royalty—American Indian, ancient Egyptian, or whatever.

A friend, Mrs. Barbara Nielson of Virginia Beach, vouches for those claims and adds that she's seen many of Victoria's trances. "Copernicus and Nostradamus have also appeared to her in the trances," says Mrs. Nielson, who also says that, when Victoria goes into a trance, she changes expression. Her features begin to resemble the person who is using her voice box to communicate. Mrs. Nielson even witnessed some of the trances in which Blackfoot communicated. "When he appears to her, her chin turns blue," she says.

Blue chin, psychic Welsh family—no matter what the characteristic, the fact remains that, after a hundred years, the enduring wish of the legendary Chief Blackfoot, Chief of all Chiefs of the Crow nation, has become reality. His remains returned to his own sacred land, he lies now and forever among his own people.

And all because of one jovial lady who had an incredible dream.

5
CAR CRIME

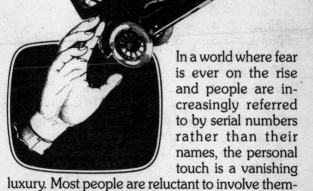

In a world where fear is ever on the rise and people are increasingly referred to by serial numbers rather than their names, the personal touch is a vanishing luxury. Most people are reluctant to involve themselves in the lives of others, and police are angered to hear, "I don't want to get involved" from more and more potential witnesses every day.

Studies have already shown that passersby are

wary of helping even a lost child who stops them on the street—one out of two people will stop, which only sounds like a lot until you give it a minute's thought.

But what about people who see a crime committed, an actual illegal act happening before their eyes? Will they do something about it, or just let it happen as if they didn't see anything?

What would you do?

Two sociologists from New York's Fordham University—Harold Takooshian and Herzel Bodinger—decided to find out. The best way to do that, they reasoned, was to stage a crime, in broad daylight, where anyone passing by could see what was going on, and see what happened.

Here's how they did it.

First, they decided to have the "crime" involve a thief and a car, since cars are such visible objects, parked by the thousands on streets everywhere. A thief breaking into a car parked on a busy thoroughfare anywhere in the country would have to attract someone's notice, and then it would be up to that someone to intervene or just stand idly by.

Next, two of Takooshian's students—Franklin (black) and Gene (white)—were asked to play the parts of the thieves. They dressed in their shabbiest clothes and reported for duty. Another student, a woman, would pose as the nicely dressed owner of the car—a white Cutlass. Two Manhattan locations were selected as study sites: one at the corner of West 74th Street and Broadway, the other at an equally busy corner, West 61st Street and Broadway.

The female student parked the Cutlass on the street, in a very visible parking space. Then, in a

THAT'S INCREDIBLE!

very noticeable way—easy for bystanders to see—she got out of the driver's seat, gathered a fur coat in her arms, and moved it to the passenger's side of the front seat. Then, after locking all the doors, she disappeared into a nearby shop.

The rest of the little drama was up to Franklin or Gene. One of the two (and sometimes both of

them together) would stealthily approach the car, looking very suspicious, peer into the car to get a good view of the fur coat, and finally take out a wire coat hanger. With the coat hanger, unbent and with a hook at one end, the "thief" would attempt to open one of the car doors in order to get at the coat.

The experiment was tried many times. Did anyone try to stop Gene and Franklin? Did anyone even ask for an explanation? The results might surprise you.

On one occasion Gene was working away, trying to open the door of the Cutlass, when a passerby stopped to see what was happening.

"Just forgot my keys," said Gene to the man leaning over his shoulder, watching him work the coat hanger. "I never had such a hard time getting a hanger. Can't seem to get it in there. Could you tell me when I get it?" The observer coached him for a minute or two. Then Gene said, "Should I turn it now?"

"A little bit more," said the "thief's" unwitting "accomplice," who'd never asked if the car belonged to Gene.

After a near miss, Gene acted a bit exasperated and turned to the stranger. "Boy, my wife's gonna kill me for this. Listen, would you just take a crack at it for me? I'd really appreciate it."

"Sure," said the stranger and took the hanger. He began to work at the inside lock and talked as he worked. "The cops, the traffic cops, they're experts at this. They do so many of them."

Much better at the coat-hanger trick than Gene, the passerby soon had the lock hooked with the hanger. "There you go!" he said as the man opened the door.

"That's why I keep two sets of keys," the triumphant stranger said, "one in the back pocket, so I've still got a set if I leave one in the car."

"Well, my wife took my spare set," said Gene.

"I'd keep it with me," the man cautioned.

"Well, I'll do that from now on," Gene said and

THAT'S INCREDIBLE!

THAT'S INCREDIBLE!

nodded. The man accepted his thanks, and as the passerby went on his way, Gene fished the fur coat from the front seat and sprinted in the other direction.

Did the passerby ever realize he'd aided and abetted a "thief"? Probably not. There was no malice in the man's actions; he just wasn't responsible for the outcome no matter what he did, so he simply tried to help.

In repeated attempts to "steal" the fur coat from the car, the thieves got away with their crime every time. And New York—where less than two percent of all street criminals are ever apprehended—was by no means the only city where this kind of experiment was tried. The car crime was staged in Baltimore, Buffalo, Toledo, Miami, Ottawa, and Phoenix. Phoenix would appear to be the safest place to park your car if it has valuables in it (or even if it doesn't): whereas the thieves were questioned only three percent of the time in a city like New York, the suspects were questioned twenty-five percent of the time in Phoenix. If questioners were few, helpers were many, and even the police offered help; they assumed the mock thieves had truly locked themselves out of their cars, then assisted with the break-ins without bothering to ask for identification or anything else!

Most often, however, onlookers neither helped nor hindered. They merely ignored what they saw.

"Originally," says Harold Takooshian, a director of the study, "we thought the best way to understand how criminals get away with their crime would be to actually simulate a crime ourselves and then observe how people react. Overall we found that only three percent of the time did New Yorkers take a sufficient interest to even question the suspect. Certainly the normal response, the most common response, is ignoring. People walk by without giving the suspects a glance. Then, about thirty-three percent of the time, passersby *notice* the suspect—but that's all they do is notice. They may watch for a second or two, perhaps even longer, but then they walk away.

"And finally there was that peculiar response that we never foresaw when we were planning this study—which is stopping to actually help the suspect. Every now and again a man would step forward and help the suspect break into the car, without ever asking any serious questions."

So this is the way onlookers would respond to a crime being committed right before their eyes. But why? Is it lack of responsibility? Perhaps immorality? Maybe even cold callousness?

Stanley Milgram,, professor of psychology at the City University of New York believes the reason stems from what he calls "adaptation to overload."

And here's what *that* means, in simpler English. In big cities an individual may encounter thousands of people in a matter of minutes, although he may not know any of them by name (in midtown Manhattan, as a matter of fact, the number is placed at an incredible 220,000 in a ten-minute period. That may be more people than there are in your entire hometown!). In order to cope with the sheer number of people he sees, an individual may simply decide, subconsciously, to just not see anything that isn't essential to his own survival. He leaves problems like poverty, illness, crime, and

THAT'S INCREDIBLE!

unemployment to the institutions equipped to handle them and avoids involvement with others, preferring to go about his own business. Thus, when he sees a crime being committed, he leaves the criminal's fate to the police—after all, he doesn't know the victim, so he won't be hurt by whatever it is the criminal is doing.

It's interesting to note, however, that that same person might very well behave very differently in a small town where he knew the people and the normal standard of behavior, and where fewer survival demands were placed on him.

Ask some of your friends. What would *they* do? Here are some replies you might hear:

"I'd see what was in it for me," said one young man.

"I'd help him," said one lady with a laugh.

"I'd ask him what he was doing," said another brave young woman. "I'd check his reaction to that, and if I didn't like it, I'd start looking for a cop."

How about a child's response? "I'd go, 'What are you doing?' and I'd yell and try to pull him away from the car." And if the thief was much bigger? "I'd still yell, and I'd grab for his feet."

One old lady admitted she'd "scream at him and tell him to leave that car alone."

But a twenty-year-old man probably is typical of most. "I'd mind my own business and keep walking."

Certainly his is the response shown by most people who witnessed the crime staged by sociologists at Fordham University. But have you decided yet what *you* would do?

Think about it.

6
ROCK OF AGES

What, exactly, is the fate of a fad? Does anyone ever really notice when a fad has run its course, outlived its usefulness, or just plain old become boring? Probably not. Hula hoops disappear—either lost or stored in the garage until, years later, the next generation pulls them out to wonder what they were ever used for. Little troll dolls get passed on to younger sisters. We stop watching *Batman* after all the plots have begun to sound the same, and the network eventually gets the message and takes the show off the air. Old fads don't seem to die, they just fade away.

Or at least that's what happens to most fads. Most fads involve a television show everyone watched (in ten years' time no one will *believe* there was so much commotion over who shot J. R.), a toy everyone bought, a word everyone used (remember "groovey"? Would you be caught dead using that word now?). But occasionally a fad comes along that involves a real, living thing, a thing you've come to know and love and that may even have come to know and love you.

What do you do when *that* fad dies?

It could happen to you—if it hasn't already. You may be one of the people who bought a pet rock, or were given one, during those months when the new breed of pet came on the market. Maybe your apartment was too small for a dog, or you were allergic to cat fur, and a parrot seemed too expensive, and thus the quiet, passive pet rock, with its nice manners and easy-care aspects, seemed just right. You put yours on your desk, where you could talk to it and ask its advice, or maybe it perched on your shelf, out of harm's way yet always within petting distance.

Californian Ed Markey was the proud owner of a pet rock named Stonie. He'd had Stonie for several happy years when suddenly something seemed strange, and Ed, ever the loving owner, began to worry that Stonie's health wasn't what it had been in happier times. He fretted, asked friends for advice, put cold compresses on what he assumed to be Stonie's forehead, even visited a

THAT'S INCREDIBLE!

helpful but inevitably helpless veterinarian, but in the end all seemed lost. Ed was all but sure that Stonie had passed over into whatever pet rocks consider the next world.

Heartbroken, Ed Markey turned his thoughts to a method of preparing Stonie for eternal rest. A local pet cemetery said it could accept Stonie as a headstone, but could not place him under one. Ed had no backyard to bury Stonie himself, and he was loathe to ask a friend to loan him grave space. And anyway, Ed was not positive Stonie was really gone. Who could he ask for help?

Help materialized in the form of an advertisement in the back of a magazine Ed was reading in an attempt to distract his grieving mind. "Has *your* pet rock died?" the ad asked, and as he read the words, Ed Markey sat upright, suddenly alert. Reading on, he read of a final resting place for pets like Stonie. Called Rocky Gardens, it featured a Memory Wall of Fame, where Stonie—if he had indeed passed on—could rest forever with pets of his own kind. The address given was in Pleasant Hill, California, not far from Ed's hometown, and he wrote Rocky Gardens a letter that night.

A few days passed, and he received a compassionate, understanding reply, asking him to come and visit the following day. If possible, Ed was to bring Stonie with him. Ed prepared Stonie for the journey, and drove to Rocky Gardens the following day.

He was met at the door by the establishment's directors, Jan and Larry Jansen. "I'm Ed Markey," said Ed when Larry extended a welcoming hand to him. "I got your letter yesterday. . ." Somehow he felt self-conscious, but the unease soon left him.

"Yes, hello, Eddie," Larry said kindly, ushering Ed into the entrance hall and gently closing the door behind him. "I'm glad you got in touch. I'm sure you did the right thing, writing to us right away."

"I hope so," Ed told him, clutching the bag—in which he'd wrapped Stonie—to his chest. "I didn't know where else to turn, so when I saw your advertisement. . ."

"Of course, of course," said Larry and motioned Ed into a chair. Then he moved quickly on to the hardest part of that initial meeting. "When did you first begin to feel that—"

"Well, he hasn't been moving the last couple of

THAT'S INCREDIBLE!

weeks," Ed explained, happy that, at last, he could share his anxieties with someone who would understand.

"Not in a long time," Larry echoed.

"Yeah, it's been a while." Ed patted the bag in his lap with obvious affection.

"Well," said Larry with a nod to Jan, "we should take a look at him right now to see what the trouble really is. Our first responsibility is to establish that he is truly gone."

"I understand," said Ed and handed the neatly tied parcel to Larry, who handed it to Jan. Jan unwrapped Stonie and held him gently in the flat of her hand, admiring his looks.

"Ah, he's a handsome fellow," Larry said, "a real beauty." He motioned to his colleague. "Jan, would you get the stethoscope so we can check this little guy out?"

She did so and attached the twin earpieces to her ears, then waited while Larry placed Stonie on a small green satin pillow. As she touched Stonie with the contact attachment, Larry explained the proceedings to the anxious Ed.

"Now, Ed," he began, "this is one of the ways that we determine if there are any vital signs. And if there aren't, of course, then we know that your rock is indeed deceased."

Ed nodded his understanding.

"Hardening of the arteries is a very common cause of deceasement here," Larry continued, while all awaited the outcome of Jan's tests. "After twelve to fifteen million years, of course, that's perfectly understandable."

Jan slipped the earpieces down and shook her head, obviously touched. "I'm sorry," she said with a sympathetic look at Ed. "I think he's really gone."

"He's gone," Larry said, as if to make it official.

"It might have been simple old age," Jan said, trying to be helpful.

"But are you *sure?*" Ed asked. He'd been dreading this moment for weeks, and now that it had finally come, he was still unwilling to accept it.

"There are other tests," Larry told him.

"Please," Ed said.

"We have the water test," Larry began and moved to an exquisite cut-glass goblet filled with the purest of spring water. "Now the theory here is that—and I believe it's true—that if your pet floats, he's all right, and if he doesn't . . ."

"I understand," said Ed.

"You needn't watch," Larry told him kindly. "It may be hard on you."

THAT'S INCREDIBLE!

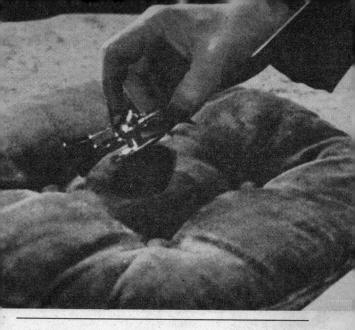

"I can take it." Ed swallowed hard but steeled himself for the outcome.

Jan gently dropped Stonie into the clear water. Without pausing for even an instant, he sank straight to the bottom.

"Looks like he's gone," Larry whispered.

"I think so, Ed," Jan agreed.

"But surely there's another chance . . ." Ed said miserably. "I wouldn't want to give up on him if any possibility still existed that he isn't, you know, deceased."

Larry and Jan looked at each other, wondering if that last step should be taken in this case, when all hope seemed truly lost. They made a decision with their eyes, and Jan fished Stonie from the bottom of the goblet. Taking a white linen napkin,

85

she lovingly dried him off while Larry braced himself for what would follow.

"There's one last thing we can do, if you want to be truly sure." His face was filled with dread. "It's considered cruel by some people, but when we feel it is imperative to erase all possibility of doubt, it's a method we are sometimes forced to resort to. If you're agreeable, I'll explain how it works."

Ed took a deep breath. "Okay," he said simply.

Larry and Jan—still cradling Stonie—led Ed to an adjoining room whose principal furniture was a large television set with a small but elegant stool placed just in front of its screen. Ed began to get an inkling of what might be about to happen, and he wondered if he could go through with it.

"To make absolutely sure the rock is dead," said Larry, "although it's cruel, we put it in front of a television game show, and if it doesn't move,

THAT'S INCREDIBLE!

doesn't in any way attempt to escape—well, then we really know beyond a shadow of a doubt that it is in fact deceased."

Jan placed Stonie in the middle of the stool, then she and Larry led Ed to an observing position behind a protective screen. Peering through the observation window, Larry pressed a remote-control button which activated the set. The screen flickered to life, and the mindless yammer typical of game shows began to blare. Seconds passed while Ed, mercifully unable to see what was happening to his beloved pet rock, wondered what was going on.

Then Larry spoke, "I don't see any movement at all, and it would appear that your rock has passed on. With a show like that, if the rock hasn't moved at all, no further tests are needed."

Larry turned to see Ed's bereaved expression.

"I'm sorry, Ed," he said. "I can't tell you how sorry I am." Jan placed a compassionate hand on his arm.

"I'm okay," Ed said in a manner not as convincing as he'd hoped. "I guess I've known this was coming. But I didn't want to give up hope."

"It's a terrible thing to lose a pet you've had for years," Larry said, attempting to distract him while Jan removed Stonie's remains to another room. "But there are arrangements to be made now, and we can help if you'd like us to."

"First I'd like to get out of this room," Ed said with a last anxious look around. He and Larry went back to the reception room and resumed their seats. "I'll leave it up to you. I'll pay whatever it costs. I want the best. Stonie deserved the best."

"Of course he did," Larry agreed. "Then shall we have the services tomorrow at, say, two o'clock?"

"That's fine," Ed said, his eyes beginning to water.

Larry handed his new client a tissue from the box he and Jan kept on the table for just such occasions. Ed accepted it gratefully.

The next day the mourners gathered, friends and relatives of Ed's who had enjoyed Stonie's presence during better days. Unkindly, nature had decided on rain as the order of the day, and thus all held umbrellas as protection against the elements. But all listened as Larry, who was officiating, read from the book he held in his hands—*Principles of Geology*—and there were no dry eyes when he began to speak.

"Dear friends," he began, "we are gathered here this morning at Rocky Gardens Pet Rock

THAT'S INCREDIBLE!

Memory Wall of Fame, to witness the enwallment of Stonie, erstwhile companion and paperweight to one of our dear clients, Ed Markey. Stonie, while he vibrated with life and harmony with his master, provided with firm affection a stolid bulwark against the vicissitudes and turmoil of our existence. His loyalty had a staunch, concrete quality about it, yet he could exhibit tenderness and could soothe and calm as does the cool, gentle touch of moss. His master—nay, his friend—mourns him and we join in sympathy at this solemn moment. Join your brethren, Stonie, sleep in peace and tranquility until the great melt-down when you will once again vibrate with every atom to the music of the spheres."

And with that, Larry troweled onto a low stone wall a small amount of soft mortar onto which the rain softly fell. Giving Ed a nod, Larry gave him his cue to place Stonie firmly in the mortar, fixing forever the rock's position in the wall. Pausing for a moment of silence on behalf of his departed friend, Ed sighed deeply, then moved away from the wall. After he had done so, each of the mourners passed by Stonie's final resting place, leaving behind as they passed their tokens of affection—single red roses.

A band played music to keep the procession moving: the strains of "Rock of Ages" lifted on the air. The service had been the best, for Stonie—who deserved only the best.

Larry and Jan Jansen's unique pet cemetery was founded in 1979, when their own pet rock, Herbie—a gift from their son—passed away. Rocky Gardens Memorial Cemetery, born out of

THAT'S INCREDIBLE!

necessity, was thus founded to help themselves and others in need during a troubled time. For just $3.79 the bereaved can know their late pets will rest forever atop that lovely semicircular wall in Pleasant Hill, California. In addition they receive a "certificate of mortar" (suitable for framing)—listing the deceased's name, age, and cause of death if it can be determined—and a color picture of the final service if they are unable to attend.

Is the touching case of Ed Markey and his Stonie the only one they have encountered since opening their cemetery? By no means.

One grieving couple sent their pet rock, Blondie, asking that she be interred "on the shady side of the wall because she sunburns easily."

Croaker, an artfully decorated rock resembling a frog, arrived for services, with a note informing the Jansens that he had—what else—"croaked."

And there have been many others. The Jansens tenderly care for all arrivals.

"We feel like we're doing a public service," Jan explains, "helping rocks pass on with dignity." Her manner suddenly turns stern. "But there's one thing we just won't do."

And what's that?

"Cremations."

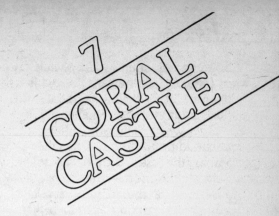

7
CORAL CASTLE

It's a story that's been told over and over again, for as long as men and women have been falling in love with each other—quite a long time—but a story that, unfortunately, becomes no less sad with each retelling. It's the story of a young man who falls in love with the girl of his dreams, woos and wins her, asks her to marry him, and listens with joy as she says "yes," then suffers the heartbreak of losing her.

Someone older and wiser always says, "Don't worry, there'll be other girls." Very often the older-and-wisers are right: time heals the pain of the loss, the boy finds and wins another girl. But there are also times when there is no other girl for the brokenhearted boy, and he spends the rest of his life mourning the loss of the girl who got away.

Perhaps the most extraordinary telling of this oft-told tale is the incredible tale of Edward Leedskalnin. Born in Latvia in 1887, he grew to young manhood and met the girl he knew he would love forever. They courted, fell in love, and when Edward asked her to marry him, she agreed. It was the greatest news of Edward's life; he knew they would be happy together for the rest of their lives. Preparations for the wedding were made, and no one guessed that anything was out of the ordinary.

But then, on the eve of their wedding, something happened. Edward never knew why, what had happened to change her mind, but his lady love changed her mind and let him know there'd be no wedding for them—not the following day, not ever.

Edward was stunned, unable to understand how she could turn on him, unable to cope with his sorrow and disappointment. Deep in his heart he knew that he would always love her, no matter how she felt about him, and he knew that he couldn't continue to live in the village where they'd grown up together. He couldn't bear to think of seeing her every day, knowing they'd never have the future they'd planned and talked

about so many dreamy hours. Edward knew he'd have to leave his village, perhaps even leave Latvia—and in the end, that's precisely what he did.

Young Edward Leedskalnin packed his things, said good-bye to his family and the dreams of happiness that had been so abruptly shattered, and sailed for America, with its promise of a new life and a new beginning. Perhaps in America he could forget the girl who had broken his heart. Or perhaps he could become a man so extraordinary that she would change her mind and come back to him. In his mind the girl became his "Sweet Sixteen," and when he spoke of her—which wasn't often, for the memory hurt too much—he used the fond nickname.

Edward soon realized there was no forgetting his Sweet Sixteen. And so when he settled in the exotic Florida City, on the edge of the Florida Everglades, he began to create what would eventually come to be called the Eighth Wonder of the World.

He began by slowly saving enough money to buy the land on which to build his wonder. And then he set down to work.

What he built, over the years, is called the Coral Castle, a home built out of coral and surrounded by landscapes studded with unbelievable coral walls, coral fixtures, coral furniture—beautiful coral wherever the glance falls. He worked on the castle until his death in 1951 at the age of sixty-four, and all those years he toiled with one thought in mind: he was building the castle that his Sweet Sixteen would return to, the one in which they would live happily ever after.

Edward Leedskalnin never gave up hoping, but his hopes never turned into reality. His castle, however, became incredibly real, and now — thirty years after his death—it attracts visitors from all over the world.

There is, to begin with, the entrance to the castle, a single, enormous slab of coral that pivots to open and close. Mounted on the axle of an old Model T Ford, it has no bearings (Leedskalnin used many old automobile parts to build his castle). The average weight of the coral blocks used to build the wall is approximately six tons apiece— roughly twice the weight of the average stone used to build the Great Pyramid of Egypt.

In the garden there are rocking chairs, each perfectly balanced and carved out of a single block of coral. Edward would cut the coral block from its quarry, move it to the spot where it would ultimately rest, and carve it just where it stood. In addition to the rocking chairs Edward also created reading chairs, contoured and comfortable, which he placed around the grounds and would drift

THAT'S INCREDIBLE!

from one to another to catch the best light.

Because he had no running water or electricity, Leedskalnin fashioned a well out of coral. The water was fresh, and filtering through the coral rock served to purify it. A set of steps, also carved from coral, descended into the well: Edward could roll back a rounded gate, walk down the steps, and store tightly fitted food-filled jars in the cold water, which became a natural refrigerator.

Near the well—so that he wouldn't have to carry his water too far—he built a bathtub, also carved from a coral block. He created the tub on two levels, so that, when the tub was filled to the first level, the water would be warmed by the sun. Next to the tub he built a coral washbasin and

THAT'S INCREDIBLE!

shaving mirror, so highly buffed that it still offers a reflection!

Elsewhere on the grounds Leedskalnin built a small stockade. When asked why he built it, he explained that if he'd married his Sweet Sixteen and they'd had children who didn't behave, he'd have put them in the stockade until they were ready to behave again. It seemed to him that half an hour in a coral stockade would be enough to make any child behave all day!

He also built something *nice* for children: a little place called the Three Bears Grotto. It was a playground area, and—as always, from coral blocks—he carved all the furniture to match the story of the three bears. Among the grotto's furnishings are the

99

Father Bear's chair, as well as the Mother Bear's and Baby Bear's, three beds, a table with three porridge bowls, all just the way they appear in the story. He even carved a small heart-shaped chair for Goldilocks, just in case she should ever decide to come back.

Leedskalnin took as much care inside the house he'd built for his Sweet Sixteen as he did on the outside. In the bedroom, for instance, are twin beds carved from coral rock, two children's beds, a cradle, and a baby rocker. A massive coral fireplace provided a fire for cooking. Carefully planned, the house had perfect cross-ventilation, plenty of fresh air, and was completely safe from Florida's famous hurricanes.

Perhaps the saddest touch in Edward Leedskalnin's Coral Castle, inside or out, is the heart table in the garden. Carved in the shape of a heart, it was surely meant as a welcome-home present for his Sweet Sixteen who would never return. And Edward built it in such a way that a natural centerpiece of Florida wildflowers would grow from the rock year round.

Now, all this elaborate carving from coral is certainly impressive, and that a jilted man—especially one so cruelly jilted—should show such devotion is touching. But why is the Coral Castle sometimes called The Eighth Wonder of the World?

The answer is simple: try though they might, even the world's greatest experts are unable to explain how Edward Leedskalnin—a small man weighing only 110 pounds—managed to move the enormous coral blocks out of the quarry from which were cut to their resting places at the castle

THAT'S INCREDIBLE!

site. He managed to raise and move stones weighing up to thirty tons, doing all the work by hand. To this day, no one is able to explain how he did it.

His tools, of course, are still at the excavation site and in his workshop, just as he left them. But the tools raise more questions than they answer. After all, in 1981 there is no machinery capable of

moving a stone anywhere near the size Leedskalnin regularly moved, using only pulleys, winches, hammers, and chisels. Very secretive about his work, he never let anyone watch him, and he left no notes that anyone has found; the result is that the Coral Castle is now one of the world's riddles, something like Stonehenge and the Great Pyramids.

Is moving a block of coral really all that hard? That's easy enough to find out without straying far from the Coral Castle.

At the Keystone Quarry in the Florida Keys, for instance, huge tractors and other machines are used to slowly, laboriously extract from the ground coral blocks weighing "only" nine tons. Even with the best modern equipment the job isn't easy, and the machine is put to the test. After all, nine tons is about the limit of what a crane can lift.

Ask a quarry worker about lifing a coral rock weighing *thirty* tons, and here's what he'll tell you: "It couldn't be done." He seems so sure.

Not even with the modern equipment?

"Not with the modern equipment," he says with just as much confidence. "I wouldn't cut more than four foot long by thirty-two inches by seven or eight foot. That's the most I would cut," he continues, then waves at the struggling crane, "and you see the trouble I have getting it out with that machine."

William Alexander, a construction engineer, has made a painstaking study of Edward Leedskalnin's work. He is most amazed by the massive entrance gate, which is at least ten feet tall and very wide.

"It's one of the engineering marvels of this place," he says with obvious admiration. "This rock weighs nine tons, and it was brought from the ground. Mr. Leedskalnin mounted this as a swinging gate, and it's so beautifully balanced that it can be pushed open with the fingertips, open up to any desired width." And as he says that, he gives the gate a little push, watching again with wonder the ease with which the gate opens.

THAT'S INCREDIBLE!

William Alexander is not the only one to take an interest in Edward's work. Neighbors also watched the progress of the Coral Castle, with great curiosity that was never satisfied.

"He used handmade tools and blocks and tackle, but he never let anyone see how he did it," says one. "That was his secret."

"He would tell you what he was going to do next, though," adds another. "He'd tell you ahead of time."

Neighbors shed some light on how the secretive Leedskalnin lived, though they can add no knowledge about his work. They point out the great steel gate that was always kept closed, and the bell rigged next to it. Visitors who were curious to know what was going on inside could ring the bell, and Leedskalnin, if he wasn't too busy with his work, would invite them in and show them around. He never charged admission, but the occasional dime or quarter pressed on him by a grateful guest was never refused. In fact, such donations were his only income.

Thus we know how Edward Leedskalnin kept himself and his work alive, but the secrets of his work, and how he single-handedly moved blocks of coral no machine could move today, were buried with him. Like Stonehenge, with its enormous stones moved hundreds of miles by a means no modern mind can imagine, the Coral Castle will no doubt remain a riddle, to be puzzled over for years and years to come.

And if the Coral Castle is a massive riddle waiting to be solved, then surely its strange creator, Edward Leedskalnin was too. When he died in 1951, the cause was listed as "malnutrition"—a

natural enough fate to befall a man who lived on nickels and dimes and what they could buy. There are those who cast aside the cause of death as it is written on the death certificate, however. They believe that, if ever a man died of a broken heart, it was Edward Leedskalnin, who went to his grave mourning the loss of a love who abandoned him forty years before.

8
SKULLPTOR

The place is northern Wisconsin. The time is autumn, 1979. Along the flat, snow-covered ground, through which sparse vegetation occasionally pokes its head, a man with a shotgun cradled in his arms walks through the clearing as leafless snow-shrouded trees loom in the background.

Dale Prinsik, a teacher in a public high school, was grouse hunting with his father-in-law that day,

October 7. He could not have known when they set out the grisly turn their outing would take. If he had, he might never have gone.

But he did go, and after several hours stalking game in the Wisconsin woods, Dale thought he'd caught a glimpse of a deer, far up ahead in the distance. When he moved closer, however—quietly, almost without sound, hoping to avoid frightening the animal away— he discovered something completely unexpected, something all the noise in the world would not have disturbed. He saw the tennis shoe first, deceptively normal against the grisly form to which it was attached. Not anxious to look closer at the ghastly sight, Dale backed away slowly, then suddenly turned and ran in the direction from which he had come.

THAT'S INCREDIBLE!

"There were two of them," Dale said, recalling the day. "One appeared to be smaller, so we just assumed that one was an adult and the other was either younger or a child."

What Dale Prinsik had discovered in the woods that day were two bodies—both partially decomposed, and both completely unrecognizable.

Marinette, Wisconsin, where the bodies were found, is in the local county seat. An investigation into the mystery was begun by Chief Deputy Robert Kohlman.

"We estimate that, when the bodies were found, they had been in the woods approximately three to ten weeks," says Kohlman, who sent missing persons teletypes throughout the state.

"The pathologist's examination," he continues,

"revealed that both victims were shot in the head and died as a result of gunshot wounds.

"We broadcast the description of the two victims to the local news media. Once they were printed, we began receiving telephone calls from people who thought they recognized the two victims from their descriptions, or else they knew of a woman and a child who had been missing in the area. We tracked all these down, but none of the leads came to anything. We've come up with nothing positive."

The police were unwilling to give up the search for the victims' identities, but how do you identify a human body when there are no fingerprints and no witnesses to the murder?

In fact, there *is* another method, and the Wisconsin police decided to give it a try. In Norman, Oklahoma, a unique method of identification is being performed by medical artist Betty Gatliff and University of Oklahoma anthropology professor, Dr. Clyde Snow.

"Dr. Kenneth Bennet at the University of Wisconsin recommended that we attempt a facial restoration. Chief Deputy Kohlman got in contact with us and sent us the skull of the adult female in February."

Working as a team, Snow and Gatliff would attempt to reconstruct from the skull the victim's facial features. With luck, the result would bear sufficient resemblance to the victim in life to allow identification by friends or relatives.

The chances for identification through facial structure aren't overwhelming, but even the slightest possibility is too great to pass up. And so far, the team's batting average has been very good. The

THAT'S INCREDIBLE!

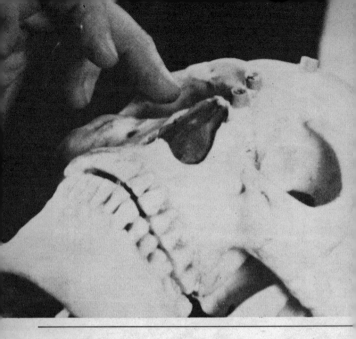

two have worked together on about thirty or forty facial reconstructions and, in the cases eventually solved, photographs of the victims showed that Gatliff and Snow had done their work with extraordinary accuracy.

About seventy percent of the cases they have worked on have been solved as far as the matter of identification goes; Snow further estimates that between fifteen and twenty-five percent of the cases have been solved as a direct result of facial reconstruction.

Facial reconstruction isn't cheap, and it takes quite a bit of time; therefore it's used when all other sources of identification have already been exhausted. The success rate of this unusual team,

THAT'S INCREDIBLE!

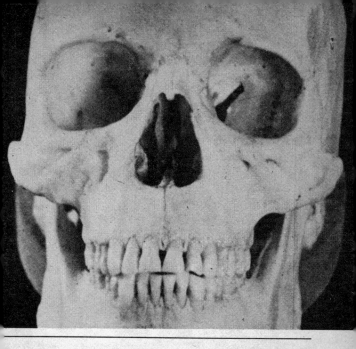

however, makes them very busy, and has kept moving around the country in order to meet the demands for their time.

The first determination Snow makes from the skull is the victim's sex and race. Betty Gatliff can't even begin to reconstruct the face unless she knows the sex of the victim. Snow also estimates the victim's age. Dental work gives Snow further clues to the victim's socioeconomic background. With all this information, Gatliff will have enough rough information to begin "fleshing out" the victim's features on the skull.

Betty's work begins with the placement of cylinders (often common pencil erasers) corresponding to the average thickness of the soft tissue over what the team calls "certain bony landmarks of the facial skeleton." Snow's determination as to the race of the victim gives them important clues at this stage. The cylinders are cut to size for both the area of placement and the composite of the individual.

"The features are based on the skull," Betty explains, "the width of the nose, the width of the mouth, the thickness of the lips, the eyes, the placement of the eyes. The eyes are centered in the orbit and aligned with the bony structure above and below the eye. Then it's a matter of tapering the clay from one depth to another. Sort of like connect the dots, if you will.

"Once I've connected all the dots, one tissue

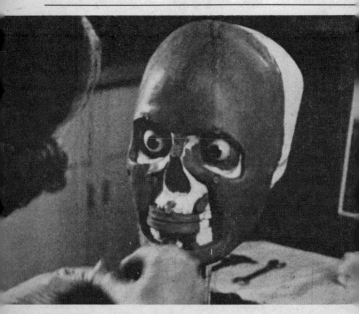

THAT'S INCREDIBLE!

depth to another, I have a framework with which to start building the features, making it look like a real face. Then I'm ready to add the mouth, connect the mouth with the chin and the cheek area."

Watching her work, one gets the feeling she's creating a strange kind of sculpture. Her tools are somewhat the same, but the process has an eerie aspect to it. Betty Gatliff seems to disregard all that, however.

"In building the eye, I try to make it as anatomically correct as I can and yet look very human. I put the lower lid in first, and it generally is straighter than the upper lid. The lower lid touches the bottom of the iris. Then the pupil seems to hang from the upper lid, which is curved." It's

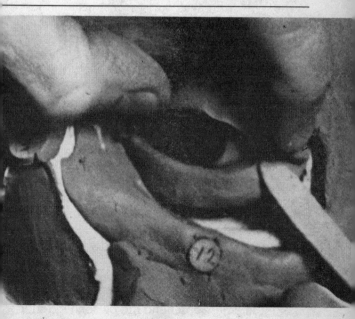

rather like putting together the same puzzle for the millionth time: it all becomes somehow automatic for her.

"The size of the nose is based on the dimensions of the nasal aperture. All of the facial features are based on the skull, so of course it's limited. I can't know about wrinkling and certain lines and so on. So I simply do what the skull tells me to do and then stop."

Finally, with the help of a bit of the victim's hair—when it's available—Betty fashions a wig for the reconstructed skull. Then the finished "face" is photographed, generally in black and white, under lighting specially designed to provide realistic skin tones.

The Wisconsin skull was reconstructed in just this way. "My conclusions," said Dr. Snow when Betty Gatliff had finished her work, "and those of Professor Bennet, were that this is the skull of an adult female probably somewhere in her upper twenties or up to forty years of age, five three to five six, white with probably a strong to moderate American Indian admixture."

In February, 1980, photographs of the reconstructed face were published, and police in Marinette kept their fingers crossed, hoping for the best. Several responses to the photographs were received, the leads were followed up, and—in a dramatic ending to the story—the woman was finally identified.

Her name was Mary Bartels, and she was from Saginaw, Michigan. The mother of two, she had died at the age of twenty-nine years. With this new knowledge, Chief Deputy Robert Kohlman could possibly, in time, apprehend the person who shot

THAT'S INCREDIBLE!

Mary Bartels and her daughter, and close the case.

What were the actual steps that led to the identity of the murdered woman? Chief Deputy Kohlman tells the story:

"Our department received information from a young man who was hospitalized in Marcut, Michigan. While there, he received a newspaper containing the photographs of the facial recon-

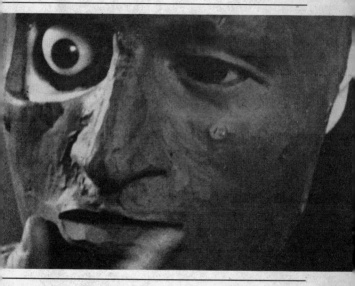

struction. He showed the photographs to several other patients at the hospital and one of them thought that she recognized the woman as a former companion of hers from Bay City, Michigan.

"We contacted the Bay City police and they—being close to Saginaw—knew that Saginaw had two 'missings' who closely resembled our victims.

So we contacted Saginaw, exchanged information, and ultimately identified our victims."

One more positive identification to add to Gatliff and Snow's already impressive statistics. Obviously facial reconstruction is a police aid with a promising future.

The likeness of the facial reconstruction to the actual appearance of Mary Bartels is uncanny, and it brings to mind a story concerning one of the Oklahoma team's earlier successes. *The Journal of Biocommunications* had run a photograph of the reconstructed face of a woman whose partially cremated remains had been found in an isolated woods in central Oklahoma. When the photograph was shown to the woman's brother, he had to be convinced that the photograph had not been taken of his sister while she was still alive.

9
EDUCATED DOGS

Which animal is tops on the intelligence scale? Is it the dolphin, which some people claim is even smarter than man? What about the monkey, which can be taught to type and even to use sign language? Maybe you'd vote for the cat—that aloof but somehow very intelligent creature.

Piedmont, Oklahoma's, Chuck Eisenmann would put his dogs up against any of the above,

119

and maybe all of them put together, in the smarts department, and you know what? His dogs would probably win the intelligence race. If it sounds amazing, just take a look at Chuck's dogs. Seeing has got to be believing.

Stop in on any ordinary afternoon, as Chuck and his dogs are coming home from the supermarket. In the back of the station wagon the dogs are sitting quietly, waiting to be let out. Chuck gets out, grabs his two bags of groceries, and his "family" of German shepherds comes spilling out behind him.

Suddenly the phone rings.

"Phone's ringing, fellas!" says Chuck, putting a spring in his step as he hustles toward the front door. He lets himself in, runs down the hall, and grabs the phone—just in time. The dogs are milling about his legs, and as he finishes his conversation, he snaps his fingers, puts the phone back in its cradle, and turns to one of the dogs.

"Hey, Toro," he says, "you know what I forgot? I left the keys in the car. Go out and get me the keys, will you, please? Atta boy, hurry up."

Toro doesn't have to think twice. He romps back down the hall, goes through the "doggie door," and runs across the yard to the station wagon. In his hurry Chuck had left the car door open, so it's no problem for Toro to reach in, grab the keys from the ignition with his mouth, and take them back into the house to Chuck.

Now, if you're one of those dog owners who'd be grateful if he could get the family dog to bring back a thrown stick, this will certainly sound unbelievable: is it possible for a dog to understand such an offhand command?

It's possible for Toro, and that's just scratching

THAT'S INCREDIBLE!

the surface of what the talented animal can do. At eight, Toro can take such commands not only in English, but also in French and German!

Unbelievable? No, just the result of the thinking of a man who sees dogs in a very unique way.

"I would say," says Chuck, "when you ask me what I'm doing with dogs, that there has to be education, and that's what I do with my dogs. I educate them. It goes beyond that which Pavlov used to talk about—conditioning an animal to the point where there was nothing else that he could do. To me, the important thing is to find an animal that is already conditioned, or else get a puppy and condition it, and then *teach.*"

When he says "teach," Chuck Eisenmann isn't using the word lightly. He has a blackboard, chalk—the works—and he and his dogs frequently sit down for work sessions on things every other school-goer knows. For instance, there's math.

"We're studying math today," Chuck tells the dogs, and on the board he chalks the number 4. "I'm writing on this blackboard a number. Could you tell me what it is?"

One dog, Hobo, obligingly barks four times.

"Right, that's four. Good boy." Chuck notices that Toro's attention is wandering, a sight familiar to every schoolteacher. "Toro, are you listening?" Obediently Toro's mind returns to the here and now, but he pays the price—the next question is his to answer. "Supposing I added this to it, Toro. If I added this to it, how many would that be?" Chuck has chalked another 4 onto the board.

Toro's lapse of attention doesn't earn him a duncecap. He thinks—yes, *thinks*—a second or two and then barks eight times.

"Right!" says the teacher, beaming at his pupils.

Chuck—also known in the world as Charles P. Eisenmann—has written two books on training dogs: *Stop, Sit and Think,* and *The Better Dog: The Educated Dog.* His methods are the result of thirty years of close living, twenty-four hours a day, with dogs, and his study of hundreds of other dog-training books. Those other books taught him plenty about training dogs, most of which centered around disregarding advice from dog-training books.

"I stopped reading them," wrote Chuck in his second book. "I felt that I had learned enough about how little the writers knew about the subject they were writing about."

Chuck's main complaint about general dog training and behavior schools is that they simply don't tap the full resources of the dog's mind, which—as Chuck Eisenmann well knows—are vast. Certainly a dog can only be as intelligent as a preschool child, but what preschool child doesn't have a vocabulary of several thousand words? What parent doesn't challenge his preschooler to

THAT'S INCREDIBLE!

think and grow and use his intelligence? Chuck treats his German shepherds just the same way, and the results are extraordinary.

In his training Chuck is extremely careful not to ask a dog to do something the dog would not, physically, be able to do. Therefore tall dogs do chores that require height, smaller dogs chores closer to the ground.

One story from his second book speaks tellingly of Eisenmann's methods and attitudes:

"I remember an appearance on the Mike Douglas TV show," he recalls. "Mike asked Hobo, one of my dogs, to place an object in the wastebasket. When he gave it to him, he placed it too deep in Hobo's mouth. Hobo, about to cough from the tickle, dropped the object on a chair, then went over to the wastebasket and put a foot in it, indicating what he was supposed to have done.

"I'm sure the action went over the heads of most of the people who were viewing, but knowing Hobo, I gave him a more desirable object and merely asked what Mike had told him to do with it. He immediately went over and put it in the wastebasket. Mentally he knew what Mike had asked, yet declined the request because he would never have gotten as far as the wastebasket without having to drop the object, so he placed it on the chair."

Chuck's faith in the dogs he regularly refers to as his "boys" has paid off well for all of them. Perhaps the only "educated dogs" in the world, his canine crew has astounded all comers. Their abilities to understand the spoken word and the uniqueness of Eisenmann's methods have brought them numerous guest appearances on such television shows as *The Tonight Show, The*

123

Mike Douglas Show, The Merv Griffin Show, and *The Today Show,* to mention just a few. The dogs have starred in sixty episodes of television's *Littlest Hobo* as well as many feature films. But Chuck Eisenmann prides himself the most in what his remarkable "boys" don't do, rather than what they can do. He has made a dog's accomplishments the rule rather than the exception.

"The success to a new approach to any problem or study," says Chuck, "lies not so much in what is said, but rather what can be shown by its application." As always anxious to show there's substance behind his words, Chuck and the dogs made over three hundred personal appearances each year for ten straight years.

For a recent appearance on *That's Incredible,* this remarkable canine corps and its innovative commander pulled out all the stops.

First, Chuck introduced the dogs, Toro and Hobo on this occasion, to their hosts. But he did it in an unusual way. "Cathy Lee Crosby is in the center," he said, "Fran Tarkenton is on her left, and John Davidson is on her right." Letting that sink in a moment, he then said, "Now, according to the way I introduced them, which one is Fran Tarkenton, Toro?"

Without missing a beat, Toro went up to Fran Tarkenton and extended a paw.

Later, after Toro had picked out random letters from the words "That's Incredible" on the show's backdrop—proving that he could easily identify letters—Chuck passed out large cards, one to each of the three cohosts.

"I have three numbers here," he said as he distributed the cards, "a 10, an 8, and a 2. Fran, you

THAT'S INCREDIBLE!

take the 10; that's your number." Each of the three held up the card provided so that the dogs and the audience could see them, and then Chuck continued.

"Yesterday, after watching him play football for years, I met Fran for the first time. While we were talking, Fran said to me, 'Chuck, there was a certain number I wore all through my playing days.'" He turned to Toro. "Toro, you were there when Fran told me what that number was. So come on, Toro, let's go, show it to me."

Again, without hesitation, Toro went straight to the number 10, which Fran was holding. Then, just to make sure no one would think Toro had been coached in advance, Chuck asked John and Fran to swap cards. When they'd done so, Chuck said, "Toro, what did I ask you to do just a minute ago? Specifically now, let's go. Show it to me." Toro went this time to John, holding the card bearing the number 10.

Next Chuck passed out name cards, but gave Fran's to Cathy Lee Crosby, Cathy Lee's card to John Davidson, and John's to Fran Tarkenton.

"Okay, Toro," Chuck continued, "which of these words is spelled F-R-A-N?"

For the first time Toro hesitated before making a choice.

"I think we got him confused," John said.

"Show it to me, Toro, hurry up," said Chuck impatiently.

The dog finally walked up to Cathy Lee, indicating the FRAN card she was holding. "I don't believe it!" she cried.

Chuck took the opportunity to point out proof that he is not coaching the dog in his answers. "I can't see the dog's eyes. You have to notice that Toro isn't looking at me. When he's thinking, he always looks away." With that explained, he went on to another demonstration. "Toro, adjacent to F-R-A-N is C-A-T-H-Y L-E-E . . ."

"You're not telling me he can spell," said Fran.

"If he knows what's good for him, he'd better," Chuck replied simply. "Toro, what did I ask you? Specifically. It's right in front of you."

The dog pointed to John, holding the CATHY LEE card.

Then, one last example of Toro's skill, "Toro, Davidson has a first name, so show me where that name is."

Back to Fran went Toro, to motion with his paw at the JOHN card in Fran's hand.

Did the three astonished cohosts believe what they saw? They had to. It was right in front of them: a dog who can read, add, speak three languages, all things most people can't do.

THAT'S INCREDIBLE!

It's all proof of Chuck Eisenmann's theory that the limit of a dog's intelligence lies far beyond the place where most dog training stops. So what's a good piece of advice to get you started training *your* dog to understand as many words as Toro?

To begin with, *talk* to your dog. According to Chuck—who ought to know—the more words you speak to your dog, the more words he'll begin to understand and the greater his vocabulary will become.

Will your dog ever learn to speak German? It all depends on whether or not *you* do!

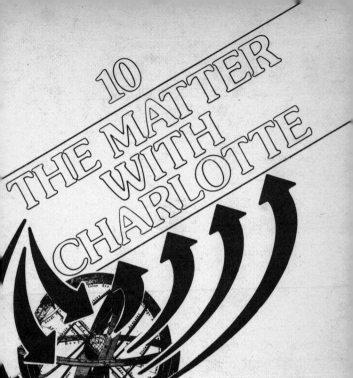

10
THE MATTER WITH CHARLOTTE

Stand on a train platform long enough, and you'll learn how to tell the train is coming long before it's in sight: there's a slight rumble you can "hear" with your feet, even if the train is still miles away. It's the vibration of faraway wheels on tracks, of course, but it's also a bit like magic, and it's fun to time yourself against a friend—to see who "hears" the train first.

Somewhere in these United States, however, is a lady who "hears" something much more amazing than an oncoming train: her name is Charlotte King, and by some extraordinary sense—that no scientist can yet explain—she possesses the unbelievable ability to hear earthquakes before they've begun, no matter where in the world they happen to be occurring and no matter how far from where she is!

Some of the earthquakes she's predicted:
August 6, 1979—Hollister, California
September 12, 1979—New Guinea
January 24, 1980—Livermore, California
March 3, 1980—Eureka, California

As if talking about predicting a mere change from fair weather to rain, Charlotte says calmly, "I've had eighty, altogether—no, make that eighty-one total—that I have experienced. All of these earthquakes have hit five or higher on the Richter scale."

She was living, as she does today, in Salem, the state capital of Oregon, when she began having these bizarre sensations. "It began about May to July of 1976," she says. "I was reading a book at home and, all of a sudden I could hear something that sounded very similar to a foghorn in the background. I kind of wondered what it was, but when I asked my husband if he was hearing the noise too, he told me he wasn't. I really didn't think much about it.

"After that, though, because I kept hearing that same foghornlike sound, I started to keep a record. I began to notice that every time I began to

THAT'S INCREDIBLE!

hear that noise, it just so happened that there was an earthquake of moderate to large intensity, somewhere in the world, within three days time.

"The newspaper here in town got wind of this kind of advance notice I was getting, and they did an article about it. Then the local television station became aware of it. They contacted me, and finally they said, 'Look, why don't you let us know the next time this happens, and we'll keep a record for you, keep track of things.' It was awfully nice of them to offer, so I took them up on it."

Doug Crombie, news editor of the station in Salem, picks up the story. "She'd give us a call when the sound began to shift, generally about two days notice. She'd be very specific, and, sure as heck

. . ." The sentence trails away; obviously Crombie himself still finds Charlotte and her special talent rather unbelievable. Although he's seen for himself that it *is* real.

"After she established the relationship with us," he continues, "she also started volunteering these sideline things about earthquakes, all of which we took as kind of background material on what was happening with her."

"They tried to test me to see how low I could hear on the decibel level," Charlotte says. "The tests showed that I can hear down to the twelve hertz range, which is quite a bit below the threshold of the normal person. Also, in the sound booth, they gave me different sounds and tried to

THAT'S INCREDIBLE!

mask the sound I was hearing out, by using what they called white or pink noise to block it. No matter what they did, though—no matter what they tried—I was still able to hear the sound without any problem."

At Oregon State University, Dr. Leland Jensen learned of Charlotte King and her unique "earthquake alarm," and asked to do some more scientific tests. Charlotte was only too happy to oblige.

Dr. Jensen gladly explains what he was able to learn, but finally is forced to admit that, at best, he is now simply capable of stating in scientific terms that he can't explain the phenomenon of Charlotte King.

"The signal we have on the oscilloscope here is

a signal that was recorded at the King's residence," he says, indicating a wavy line on a complicated-looking machine. "It's an acoustic signal obtained with a high-level or highly sensitive microphone capable of recording signals down in the order of one cycle per second." He looks at the oscilloscope, then gives his "final diagnosis": "I don't think there's any doubt that she's hearing something. Whether it is an earthquake, or whether it is some type of acoustic phenomenon, I don't know."

All of which just goes to prove that science isn't *always* standing on the sidelines with the answer to every question. But even if that strange buzz is still going on in her ears, Charlotte is taking the situation in stride.

"I really don't know what it is," she says with a good-natured shrug. "I sometimes wonder if, perhaps, the tremors of earthquakes actually begin, maybe, seventy-two hours, or even longer, before they actually begin to register on anyone's equipment, before anyone could guess there was actually an earthquake occurring."

If that is true, then Charlotte is the living proof of it, as Tom Brown, of the local Salem television station, readily admits.

"After talking to Charlotte for about two years to two and a half years, I believe she's been right something like sixty out of sixty times she's made a report to us. What that says to me is that she manages to get all of them —small ones and big ones. And, I'd say within the last six months, she's getting it down to a fine science. These days she's been very good at getting the direction, too. Every time she calls us up, sure enough an earthquake

THAT'S INCREDIBLE!

goes down, and we all say, 'She's right again.'"

Doug Crombie, still unable to believe what he sees, remains a sort of holdout. "I've been really skeptical about it," he says. "I don't, to this moment, believe that it's happening."

Tom Brown, like most other station employees, is willing to believe the evidence he's seen over and over again. "When Charlotte calls and says there'll be an earthquake, I believe it's actually happening."

Charlotte, of course, has no choice but to believe. "I believe that there is something to it," she says. "I don't know what I'm hearing, or why I'm hearing it, or where it's coming from or why. All I know is that it's there, and the accuracy shows it works."

135

How, exactly, does it happen? Charlotte explains:

"I hear a sound, and it is by the intensity, and the frequency in rhythm of this sound, and the particular sounds that come through, that I've been able to pinpoint on some of the earthquakes. The sound becomes much more intense in loudness, and it becomes much more frequent in rhythm, when I'm receiving earthquake warnings. The tones become closer and closer together."

Recently, in addition to the varying sounds Charlotte hears, she's also begun to experience extreme headaches and earaches when an earthquake warning is under way. Does this mean there is a *super*earthquake about to occur in some portion of the world? Or does it simply mean that Charlotte King's head is beginning to show signs of strain, having experienced over eighty earthquakes in little more than four years? No one knows. We'll just have to wait and see.

But in the meantime, as quakes—large or small—occur somewhere on earth, Charlotte King will continue to hear them far in advance of their occurrence. Is it a useful skill, or just a nagging feeling she simply can't do anything about? Well, more than one California resident, having weathered that quake-torn state's tremors, has asked Charlotte to give him a call next time she gets blips on her quake warning line.

Could be that Charlotte King might become the world's first Dial-a-Quake service!

11
THE LOUDEST WHISPER

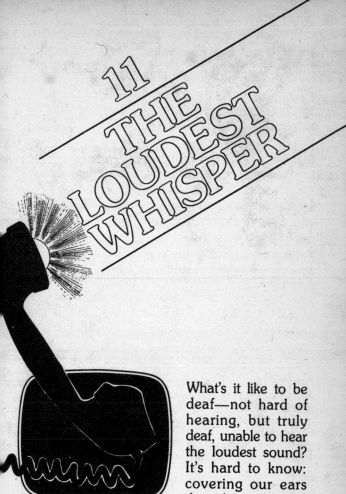

What's it like to be deaf—not hard of hearing, but truly deaf, unable to hear the loudest sound? It's hard to know: covering our ears doesn't mask it all out, nor does the best set of earplugs. And even if such attempts worked, those of us who've had the ability to hear all our lives would have our memories. We've all thrilled to the sound of the crowd's roar at a baseball game, wondered at the intrica-

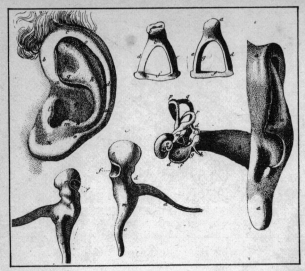

cies of the music of Johann Sebastian Bach. We know the sounds of our parents' voices. Those memories might fade with time, but the experience would always be there.

But what about those who've been deaf since birth, or soon after, people who have no memories? Could you describe, with unspoken words or sign language, the things you've heard to someone who can't even grasp the concept of sound? Such attempts have been made for years. There is even a form of sign language whose purpose is meant to teach the deaf the meaning of music.

Until now, little more than stop-gap measures could be used to make deaf people "hear." Now, however, there is an extraordinary scientific breakthrough credited with the miracle of bringing sound to the ears of many people who'd never in their lives been able to hear.

THAT'S INCREDIBLE

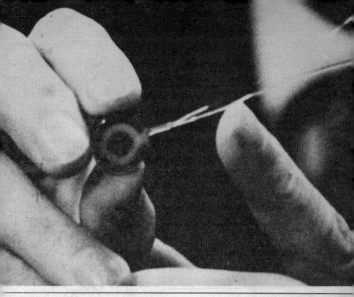

The cochlear implant seems incredibly tiny to represent such a medical miracle, but a miracle it truly is. Looked at up close, it looks like a shirt button with tiny protruding wires, its round base being no larger than a dime. One of the wires connects to a small stimulator pack, which the wearer of the implant carries with him. It's a little bit like a hearing aid, only far more revolutionary.

Dr. William House, director of the Ear Research Institute in Los Angeles, explains the significance of the medical breakthrough, developed at the institute:

"The part I'm holding here," he says, indicating the dime-sized implant, "is the portion that is actually implanted into the patient—into the part of the inner ear called the cochlea—during a surgical operation. There are also some nerve fibers that can be stimulated by electrical signals, and these give us the ability to—by putting in electric currents, *complex* electrical currents—make the patient have the sensation of sound.

"I think that, if we were to try to put the implant program in perspective, if we could compare it to the history of flight, starting with the Wright Brothers—when they actually got off the ground—and the 747 or the Concorde, I'd have to say we've probably arrived at about the place where Charles Lindbergh would be."

He's confident that his research can go all the way. "Of course it's going to take a lot of money," he says frankly. And what research doesn't? "It's also going to take a lot of effort in terms of long clinical trials. But I see all this on the horizon. Right now I know that we're very encouraged by what's happening right now. We're going to make it, in maybe the next ten or fifteen years."

Ten or fifteen years? That may sound like a long time to you, but the deaf of the world are anxiously waiting for the day. Some have already received this early model and are living new lives as a result of the surgery and the implant.

One such patient is Dennis Calley. Deaf since birth, he became a candidate for the ear implant and received one when he was in his mid-thirties. For a young man who'd never heard a sound in his life, the difference is now startling. Tests done since the implant show that Dennis can now differentiate between sounds. For the first time in his life Dennis Calley turns when his name is called, even when he is unaware there is someone in the room. It's nothing short of a miracle. Work is being done to improve his speech, and—although it has yet to be perfected—he's still working on it, and in addi-

THAT'S INCREDIBLE!

tion he's learning to play the piano. He's not ready yet for Bach, but his ability to perform a simple harmonic accompaniment is amazing.

The experience of twenty-seven-year-old Tom Bledsoe is different in some ways, but in other ways remarkably similar.

For most of his life Tom had lived in a world of complete silence. It's a world few of us know, and if—for some reason—we experience it even briefly, we find that deadly quiet world haunting. Tom Bledsoe had grown used to it.

Tom was born partially deaf, and as he grew up, his hearing gradually worsened. For many years he wore a hearing aid to make the most of what was left to him, but after a while it was no longer of any use to him. By the time he was twelve years old, Tom Bledsoe was totally deaf. His life, for the

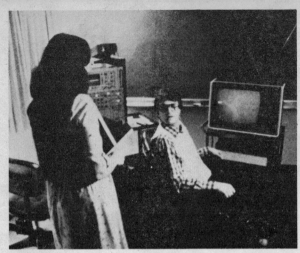

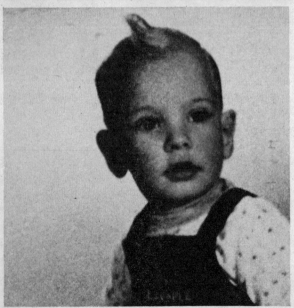

THAT'S INCREDIBLE!

next fourteen years, would be lived in a world into which no sound penetrated.

The wonders of technology normalized Tom's world somewhat, and he adapted well. A light on his telephone told him when it was "ringing." When he picked up the receiver, a machine translated the voice at the other end into writing. Using the keyboard, Tom could then respond, and in that way keep up his end of the "conversation."

But, although machines like the telephone typewriter were invaluable aids for Tom Bledsoe, they nevertheless could not provide for him the sensation of actually hearing the sounds himself. Tom wanted that sensation more than anything else in the world.

For that, Tom would need the ear implant device developed by Dr. William House at the institute.

"We have known for a long time that this would work," says Dr. House. "Now our whole problem was, clinically, with deaf people, to be able to get wires into the inner ear that would be tolerated and not rejected by the body. Our second problem was to be able to get in the very complex electrical signals that would make the sound into something that was meaningful and identifiable to the patient."

These problems were eventually surmounted. The resulting implant was surgically inserted behind Tom Bledsoe's ear when he was twenty-six years old—after fourteen years in his silent world. Once the internal device was actually implanted into his ear, then an external coil was placed over the dime-sized inner coil, *outside* the skin. By a magnetic coupling there is a current generated

143

from the outside coil to the inside coil. Sound a bit like the Six Million Dollar Man? It should!

Soon after the operation Tom Bledsoe was tested at the institute to see if the implantation would be a success. For some, the coil is unsuccessful, and everyone present was nervously awaiting the outcome of Tom's surgery. Would this deaf boy be able to hear again?

An assistant said to Tom, as she motioned to a machine, "When you hear three tones, raise your finger, okay?"

Tom read her words by watching her lips. He nodded his understanding of the instructions.

Moments passed, as Tom concentrated as hard as he could. The machine hummed—a sound the hearing spectators had no difficulty detecting. Suddenly a smile appeared on Tom's face, and with a look of triumph he raised a finger.

Tom Bledsoe could hear!

His feelings at that moment, as he described them later, were—to coin a phrase—"That's incredible!"

So, now that the implant is successfully in place, what happens to Tom Bledsoe?

Work. A *lot* of work. The implant is a tool, and—like any tool—it benefits only those who know how to use it.

The principal benefit of the implant, at its present stage of development, is a dramatic increase in the user's ability to hear the sounds being made around him. Unfortunately it does not yet enable clear discrimination—or understanding—of speech through hearing alone. Lipreading and sign language remain extremely important to the user's life.

The implant does, however, make many users much more effective in lipreading, probably because it improves the deaf person's methods of detecting the rhythm of speech. Some implant users can relay and receive simple, codelike messages on the telephone.

By the fall of 1979, the Ear Research Institute had placed ear implants in fifty-two patients, most of them since 1974. In 1975, when clinical implant research began to move more quickly, the Walt Disney Hearing Rehabilitation Research Center was established by the institute to devote its attention solely to the implant.

To date, most recipients of the ear implant have been able to use the tiny miracle and make significant changes in their lives. Tom Bledsoe, deaf for fourteen years, continues to learn the many ways his implant can make him a part of the world in which people respond to sound.

The dream of Dr. William House is an implant that will provide not just an aid to hearing and differentiating between sounds, but an implant that will allow the deaf to hear as well as those whose hearing was never impaired.

He'll get there. All he needs is time.

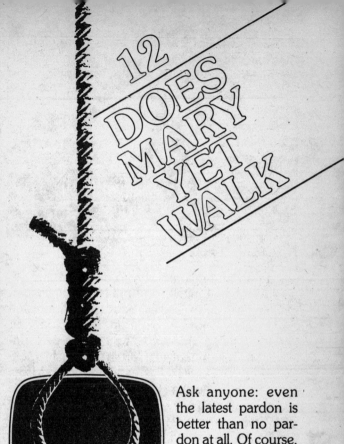

12

DOES MARY YET WALK

Ask anyone: even the latest pardon is better than no pardon at all. Of course, there's also the matter of the pardon that just happens to come when you've been dead for a hundred years ... Whoever heard of such a thing? Well, if you're at a loss, take for example the 1979 pardon of Dr. Samuel Mudd by President Jimmy Carter. He was convicted well over a hundred years ago of conspiracy, for his al-

147

leged part in the conspiracy to assassinate President Abraham Lincoln, on April 14, 1865. On that night, actor John Wilkes Booth—a disaffected Southerner—shot Lincoln from behind the chair in which the President was watching a performance of *Our American Cousin* at Washington, D.C.'s Ford's Theater. The assassin jumped from the balcony onto the stage and escaped into the night. In jumping to the stage, Booth broke his leg, which was supposedly set later by his coconspirator, Dr. Samuel Mudd.

In the years that followed the assassination Dr. Mudd's part in the conspiracy to kill the President was hotly debated. There were those who said he'd had nothing whatsoever to do with it.

Finally, in 1979, the long-sought-for pardon was granted.

Someone else, however, has yet to be as lucky as Dr. Mudd. Her name was Mary Surratt, and she too was convicted of conspiracy in the assassina-

THAT'S INCREDIBLE!

tion. There are those who say the evidence that led to Mary Surratt's conviction was as flimsy as that which trapped Dr. Samuel Mudd.

There was, however, one large difference in their fates: Samuel Mudd was exiled to Shark Island, while Mary Surratt, soon after the assassination, was hanged—the first woman in American history to die at the end of the federal government's rope.

Those who defend Mary's honor, even to the present day, swear that she was sent to the gallows, condemned to death by the testimony of a notorious liar and a habitual drunk. Who is right? Was Mary Surratt a willing partner to the assassination of one of this nation's most beloved presidents? Or was she simply in the wrong place at the wrong time, convicted of guilt by association rather than true guilt documented by reliable evidence?

Perhaps, just as Dr. Mudd's soul must now lie easier with the news that the much-maligned doctor has been pardoned, Mary Surratt's still tosses with the injustice of her death. There is, as a matter of fact, some evidence that Mary's ghost is still crying out for justice from the great beyond. That evidence comes from a reliable source: an officer in the United States Army.

According to Lieutenant James Droskinis, the apparition of a woman in a long dark gown—which he believes to be the ghost of Mary Surratt—has been moving through the rooms of his home, which, coincidentally, includes the converted courtroom in which she was convicted a century ago.

For over two years Droskinis and his wife, Kathy, lived in a five-room apartment on the third

THAT'S INCREDIBLE!

COMPLIMENTS OF THE LIBRARY OF CONGRESS

floor of a building on the grounds of Fort McNair, in Washington, D. C. Many of those buildings on the fort grounds have long and rich histories, but none has the eerie reputation of the building in which Jim and Kathy lived.

Weird things began to happen to the Droskinises the first night they spent in their apartment, the converted courtroom, in August, 1977.

They woke to hear murmuring voices, a strange and muted sound which Droskinis likened to "a crowd off in the distance." No distinct words or phrases were audible, just the steady hum of words around the bed.

The apartment was the first home of the couple's first child, Eric, born only a few months after the Droskinises moved into the apartment. The strange incidents did not stop with his birth.

One night Eric awoke, crying, and Jim went in to soothe the baby back to sleep. As he was doing so, he felt a hand on his shoulder, and even as he felt the touch, Eric fell peacefully to sleep. Happy the ordeal had been a short one, Droskinis went back to the living room, where he and Kathy had been watching television.

"You've got a magic touch," he said to her, smiling.

"What do you mean, 'magic touch'?" she asked, thoroughly confused.

"You know, when you came in," he said, sitting down and putting his feet up.

"Came in where?"

"Eric's room. Just now. Come on, Kathy, it was just two minutes ago."

"Jim," she said, deadly serious, "I've been here all the time. I don't know what you're talking about."

"Are you trying to tell me you didn't come in and stand behind me while Eric was crying, touch me on the shoulder, and then come back out here before I did?"

"Don't look at me like *I'm* the one who's imagining things!"

"If it wasn't you, then who was it?" asked Jim, bewildered.

"I don't know," Kathy replied.

It was only one of many such incidents, the first of the incidents around baby Eric. On another occasion Jim was again brought to a wakeful Eric's room. This time, as he stood by the baby's crib, he heard the sound of a rattling chain behind him. Assuming it was the sound of the Droskinises' German shepherd dog, checking the situation for

THAT'S INCREDIBLE!

itself, Jim quieted his son and rejoined Kathy. When Jim mentioned the dog, however, and its chain collar which perhaps rattled loudly enough to wake the baby, Kathy again set him straight.

"That dog's been asleep for a couple of hours, Jim," she told him. "It wasn't the dog in Eric's room."

When he began to get to the bottom of the mysterious sounds in his home, Jim learned that, during the Lincoln conspiracy trial, the seven male codefendants had been shackled with chains. They were seated in a row, very close to the spot on which Eric's crib stood.

153

During the summer of 1978, night owl Jim was nailing carpet in the hallway at about two o'clock in the morning. Suddenly he looked up to see a figure in a long dress leave his bedroom and move into the bathroom. Shrugging, he automatically assumed the late-night pilgrim to be Kathy—at least until he found her sound asleep in their bed, where she'd been all the time.

"I was amazed," said Jim later. "I checked the bathroom, but there was no one there." It hit him then, the cause of the commotion in the house. Speaking of the night he felt a hand on his shoulder in Eric's room, he said, "If I'd turned around to say 'thanks' and hadn't seen Kathy, what would I have seen?"

Possibly—just possibly—the restless ghost of Mary Surratt.

Laura Frey, wife of an army major who has lived in the apartment below the former courtroom, relates experiences of her own, some of them as incredible as those of the Droskinises. She once entered her hallways to face a woman, wearing a long dark dress, who simply stared at her.

"I immediately thought: 'It's Mary Surratt,'" she recalls. "I knew of the history of the post, and knew she had been tried and sentenced in the courtroom above us. I didn't get the impression of her face . . . . It was like I was staring through smoked glass.

"I could sense nothing unfriendly about her," she adds. "I don't know why I didn't scream or do something. Something kept me calm."

Don't get the impression that Kathy Droskinis has been left out of this ghostly situation, because she hasn't. As a matter of fact her special run-in

THAT'S INCREDIBLE!

with the spirit—or spirits—that reside in her apartment may be the most frightening of all.

One time, she was in the bathroom washing and "a whole shower of sparks came shooting down" from the wiring attached to the light above. "I was okay," she said, "just a little startled."

Rumors have for years said that the house is indeed haunted by the ghost of Mary Surratt. The history of the house has been studied and documented by the head of the Mary Surratt Society, Joan Chaconis.

"The scene of the trial was in the very building you see today in Fort McNair, on the third floor," she explains. "The prisoners' docket ran from the center window on the third floor—which is the bathroom area today—back toward the bedroom area. Mary Surratt herself actually sat just about inside where that center window is, which would be the bathroom doorway.

"Opposite the military commission was a long table that seated the reporters and also those who were visiting the trial. That would be the long hallway.

"All of the conspirators were found guilty. Four were sentenced to death. Of those four, one was the lone woman, Mary Surratt. They were brought out into an area about twenty feet from the building, where a scaffold had been built. The area was then a large courtyard, surrounded by a high brick wall."

As Joan Chaconis speaks, the solemn, terrifying scene becomes almost crystal clear in the listener's mind. "The courtyard was filled with people. The topic of conversation was probably, 'Are they really going to hang Mary Surratt today?' Would they really hang an innocent woman? Most people felt she *was* an innocent woman, just a victim of circumstance. The people who filled the courtyard that day waited for the stay of execution, but of course it never came.

"The general gave the orders, and the conspirators, all four of them, were hanged."

There Mary Surratt's earthly story supposedly ended, but, to hear Kathy Droskinis tell it, there's more.

"As I was sitting at the dining room table, reading the paper one evening, I was half-facing the kitchen. Out of the corner of my eye I could see our dog. She was in the kitchen, but suddenly I saw her sort of come out of the kitchen backward. She was propelled, slightly above the ground, as though someone had reached under her neck and shoved her back."

But, like all military hitches, the Droskinises' time as residents of the courtroom that had convicted Mary Surratt finally came to an end. None the worse for wear, Jim and Kathy and Eric finally moved away from the haunted apartment in early 1980.

Not that the ghost of the long-dead lady went without houseguests for long: new tenants moved in soon after Jim and Kathy moved out. Captain Angel Cruz, his wife Beverly, and their baby—perhaps Mary enjoys the company of three-person family groups!—are the new tenants of the third-floor officers' quarters. Will they experience the strange and haunting events that Jim and Kathy Droskinis reported during their stay in the house?

According to Captain Cruz, the first night he and his family spent in the apartment was un-

THAT'S INCREDIBLE!

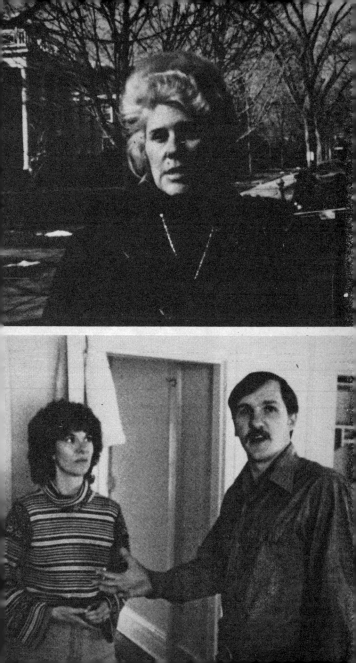

eventful, unlike Jim and Kathy's. With all the confidence typical of an army man, Captain Cruz is willing to give the apartment, and any unexpected occupants, a chance.

"I want to see what happens," he says. "I got a few years in this place. I'll wait and see what happens."

13
ADVANCE REGISTRATION

It's happened to us all. We know the phone is going to ring before it does. We know who's at the door when we couldn't have known, really, by any logical means. Such feelings are called premonitions—knowing what's about to happen before it does.

Has it happened to you?

"Unfortunately, yes," says one woman when

asked that question. "My husband and I had gone to the grocery store and we encountered a couple from our own parish. When I saw the gentleman, I had to look away, because I realized the man was going to die—I cannot tell you why. I was scared to death. And then we walked away, and I told my husband, after we went outside, about what had crossed my mind. Then, the next morning, it was announced in church that the man had died."

Incredible? Exactly. Here's another:

"Mine was in a dream. I had a dream about my husband being in an accident. I saw him coming up an on ramp, I saw a truck coming through—and then I saw them meet. In the dream I felt myself sigh with relief, and I felt okay about it, as if I knew my husband was going to be okay, and I saw him swerve. It looked like he'd brought the car under control.

"I never told my husband about it, but three days later he called me and said, 'Guess what, I was just in an accident.' And I said, 'Are you okay?' And he said, 'Yeah, I'm okay.' I said, 'Well, tell me about it,' and he told me about it, and it was exactly the same. It had been raining, and he saw the truck, and he came out of it okay. It was the same."

Luckily the woman's husband lived, but sometimes the outcome isn't so happy—such as young David Booth's dream of a jet airplane crash. He had the same terrifying dream ten nights running, and at the end of ten days—on May 25, 1979—American Airlines flight 191 crashed outside Chicago's O'Hare Airport, killing almost three hundred persons. And it happened just the way David Booth had said it would.

Some people are greeted only with laughs

THAT'S INCREDIBLE!

when they tell friends of a dream or fleeting thought in which something takes place, and later, in real life, that something actually takes place. In some ways, such responses are understandable. After all, how can we know something before it happens? Is it possible, or are people who claim to have premonitions simply trying to attract attention? Perhaps David Booth would today be greeted with laughs when he speaks of his ten dreams, were it not for the fact that, days before the plane crashed, he contacted representatives of the Federal Aviation Administration and told them about the dreams. There was nothing they could do about the dreams, although they evidently took David seriously. If they thought David's claims were funny—and there is no evidence that they did—no doubt the laughter stopped when they received word of the crash of flight 191. David Booth went on record with his premonition, and the future he foretold came to pass—giving added weight to the possibility that premonitions do in fact exist.

If your premonition doesn't fall under the jurisdiction of the FAA, of even if it does, there is a place where you can register *your* premonition, so that if your premonition comes to pass, all will know you were sincere. And perhaps, if you repeatedly foretell the future accurately, your talents can be put to good use.

That place, in New York City, is called the Central Premonition Registry, a unique project that tests the notion of foretelling the future. It is devoted to the collection and registration of dreams.

Robert Nelson, founder and director of the Central Premonition Registry, tells more about it:

"In a working week," he says, "the CPR gets all kinds of letters from all over the country, giving us the contents of dreams and visions. And of the predictions, some of them—some of them—are absolutely unusual and some absolutely disastrous. What we look for in these letters is a kind of consistency. We look for a person with more than one hit—more than one occasion on which his premonition actually translated into a true future incident."

This doesn't happen often, but Robert Nelson is quick to mention one particular registrant, whose premonitions regularly hit their mark.

THAT'S INCREDIBLE!

"We do have one person," says Nelson, "with more than one hit. As a matter of fact, he's had six really good hits in the area of airplane disasters. He prefers to remain anonymous, so we give him a code name—Greywolf."

Sound incredible? Well, seeing is believing: the Central Premonition Registry keeps meticulous records, and Robert Nelson gladly exhibits pages and pages of news clippings which document events foretold by Greywolf in his letters—all of which are carefully registered and preserved.

On May 9, 1969, for instance, Greywolf wrote the registry a letter in which he predicted the crash of a small plane. In his letter he included a list of several numbers which had figured in his vision of the plane crash. The registry logged in his letter and waited patiently to see what would happen— if Greywolf's prediction would materialize as a real event.

A few months later on September 1, 1969, an article in *The New York Times* chronicled the tragic death of prize fighter Rocky Marciano in the crash of a small plane.

163

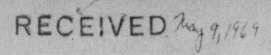

RECEIVED *May 9, 1969*

MAY 12 1969

CENTRAL
PREMONITION
REGISTRY.

[handwritten letter, partially legible] ...the thought image that followed ...appeared to be a Piper type ...was painted blue and the ...29 N or N29 N. I saw the plane t...

Careful scrutiny of pictures of the crashed aircraft revealed a truly amazing coincidence—if indeed it could be called a coincidence: the registration numbers stenciled on the plane in which Rocky Marciano crashed were remarkably similar to the numbers which Greywolf had included in his letter to the Central Premonition Registry, the numbers he had seen in his vision.

Greywolf lives in a secluded home, in a rural area of upstate New York. Somewhat desolate in appearance, the house lends itself to meditation, the kind of thoughts into which premonitions might intrude. Greywolf himself sits in front of a roaring fire in a massive fireplace as he discusses his remarkable gift.

"When it first started happening to me," he be-

THAT'S INCREDIBLE!

... and was to the thought
I saw what appeared to
sudden was pointed was for
29 N or N 29 N or N 29 N
and it appeared to be in ...
seemed to be in a mountain
could see that an emergen...

gins, referring to his visions, "I thought I was going insane. I mean, here was something I certainly never expected. These things, they come straight out of the clear blue sky and hit me right between the eyes. And then, when one of these premonitions actually came true, I just couldn't believe it. I said to myself, 'Why me?' I mean, there was never anything special about me before, and because of that, when it first started to happen to me, the very first thought I had was that I must be going crazy."

Certainly many people must doubt their sanity when they have dreams or visions that foretell the future. Others who have faith in such visions may be made to doubt their sanity by those in whom they confide. Greywolf's fears for his sanity must have been dispelled by the first 'hit'—the news

165

that one of his predictions had come true. It was not happy news, to be told that he had foretold the death of Rocky Marciano. But at least it meant he was still sane!

"I felt kind of bad, because it meant that I'm seeing things I have no control over," he continues. "And when I try to get people to listen to me, and I get nowhere at all with them, the whole thing is so frustrating I just want to blow my top. But then I found the registry, and I wrote them a letter. The simple fact that now I had someone to write to, someone to send my premonitions to and have them registered officially, helped a tremendous amount because it helped me come to terms with myself. It helps me immeasurably just to know that all I can do is the best that I can."

Above and beyond registering his predictions, knowing that somewhere a record has been made of the future Greywolf foretells—so that if he "hits," his honesty or sanity is not in question—what else does it mean to have this rare and extraordinary and no doubt frightening gift, an ability to know in advance the events of the future?

"This is something that God, nature—or whatever, whoever the Supreme Being may be—has given us. We've neglected it because we've learned how to speak; we've got television and we've got radio. But it seems to me that our ancestors must have had this to survive. I would never give up my ability." There is an extraordinary earnestness and sincerity in his voice. You know he means every word he says.

Leafing through pages and pages of materials that authenticate Greywolf's incredible predictions, Robert Nelson says the search for people

THAT'S INCREDIBLE!

with Greywolf's gift is far from over. It is, in fact, just beginning.

"We're looking for anyone who's willing to take the time and really has the desire to participate in this project, in order to find out whether or not they're truly dreaming in the future," he says. "What we're *not* looking for is professional psychics, but rather anyone out there who feels that he or she has this particular talent and would like to join us in this experiment. All it involves is keeping careful track of your dreams at night, keeping a notebook right by your bed in order to record the nature and content of your dreams. Then, when there's a genuine feeling that the dream contained something that's going to happen in the future, that's when the dream is submitted to us."

It seems simple enough. And it is not idle curiosity that made Robert Nelson start the Central Premonition Registry.

Greywolf says it best. "I know, people say that if you help avert something and keep it from happening, then there's no way it actually could have happened and there's no way you ever saw it happening.

"But I believe that what we see, however we see it, is gonna happen just the way we saw it if we don't do something to keep it from happening. Why won't it happen, if the circumstances stay the way they are?"

And it's as simple as that.

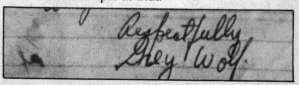

14
ENDLESS MANSION

Sarah shivered under her cape and looked with wondering curiosity at her companion. Why wasn't she cold? Sarah herself thought she might freeze to death, here in this chilly New Haven, Connecticut, sitting room, unwarmed even by the glowing fire with flames that licked ever higher in the fireplace. Her companion seemed not to notice the frosty air, but beneath her cape Sarah

169

rubbed her benumbed arms with fingers she could no longer feel.

Why had she come here, anyway? Sarah cleared her mind only to regret the memories that again became visible to her mind's eye. She wasn't young, but she had been through so much, all of it unhappy, as if someone somewhere could not abide the notion of a happy Sarah. Everything had seemed so promising when she married William—bright, handsome, rich beyond words. They had had a perfect newlywed life, and the birth of baby Annie Pardee had made them a family. But five weeks later a strange and rare illness, marasmus, so seldom seen that doctors had scarcely known how to deal with the sick infant, had taken Annie away. The coffin was tiny and white, laden with flowers, and Sarah had thought that day that she could never live through another burying.

How soon the next one had followed, and how close Death had chosen for his victim! Only a few years later her beloved William had fallen into the dark one's hands, never to return to Sarah again. Her black mourning clothes—wasn't it only yesterday that the servants had packed those dark, grief-sodden clothes away?—emerged from the attic trunks. Once again Sarah stood by a freshly dug grave and leaned on a comforting arm as a part of her life was buried forever.

"Why?" she asked friends, and then the tears would come again. "Why Annie? Why William? I'm left alone here, with no one, nothing." The $20 million William had left her was cold comfort, as were the confused responses friends gave to her questions.

THAT'S INCREDIBLE!

Cold. Yes, it was cold in that room. The chill brought Sarah's mind back to the present, and her attention returned to her companion, a woman who had traveled all the way from far-off Boston at Sarah's request. Sarah had heard the woman possessed the power to answer questions no one else could answer. Her sources were from planes few people could reach, and Sarah had asked her to come to New Haven because living with the grief, the confusion, the utter hopelessness of it all, had become intolerable. And . . .

"Mrs Winchester . . ."

Sarah heard a voice, remembered her companion, and looked to find the lady from Boston whispering her name, fluttering her fingers in the air as if playing a pair of unearthly flutes. "Mrs. Winches-

171

ter . . ." Was this the voice of the woman she had met only minutes ago? Sarah didn't think so; this voice was deeper, and there was a touch of anger in it.

"There are souls," said the woman, "thousands of souls, in pain, lost, taken from this earth before their time." A finger jabbed in Sarah's direction, so suddenly that Sarah jumped in alarm and forgot the chilly cloud that surrounded her. "They are looking at you, Mrs. Winchester. You are responsible, you and your family, your husband, his father, the Winchesters and their rifle, that cursed instrument of death and devastation . . ."

Sarah swallowed hard, but the knot in her throat would not go down. The seeress spoke of the famous Winchester Repeating Rifle, manufactured by William's father. The rifle and the money made from its sale to thousands had earned the gun the nickname of "the rifle that won the West," and at the same time created the fabulous Winchester fortune. There was no imagining the number who might have died at the wrong end of the fatal Winchester contraption.

"The souls scream," continued the Boston seeress. "They cannot rest." Strange, empty eyes leveled themselves at the now frightened Winchester heiress. "And they will not let *you* rest, Mrs. Winchester. Never."

"Never?" Sarah pressed white knuckles to her mouth. "But why me? It wasn't my rifle, it was William's father's!"

"No matter," replied the seeress in her strange voice. "They are all gone—William, Annie, old Winchester, they are all gone now to join the souls

THAT'S INCREDIBLE!

they sent early to the grave. All gone now. There remains only you."

A scream caught itself in Sarah's throat.

"Then the spirits will take me too?" she whispered.

The seeress nodded wordlessly.

"How? When?" It had always seemed to her that life without William and their infant Annie was no life at all. But now, as Death spoke her name for the first time, suddenly she wanted desperately to live.

Whistling noises rose from the seeress's throat before she said, "You need not die. There is a way."

"What way? What can I do?"

Once again the eyes turned on her, and Sarah forced herself, for an instant, to look deep into them. Her gaze traveled far down, she seemed to be staring into an abyss no scientist would ever measure. Pierced with terror but unable to pull her eyes away, she gasped, "How?"

"Build," the voice told her. "Build a house where restless spirits may dwell, the many thousands of spirits of the dead your family made. Never stop building, for there will never be room enough. Never stop building for you will never know when the last spirit has come to live with you. Never leave the house, never stop building. As long as you build, your life is safe. Stop building and the homeless spirits will come for you as they did for your husband and your daughter. Never stop building . . ."

Sarah could listen no more. She stood, gathered her skirts, and ran screaming from the room. For Sarah Winchester, widow of the late William

Wirt Winchester, the nightmare was only just beginning, in the year 1881.

Did Sarah Winchester actually believe what the seeress had told her? It's hard to say. If she did, she came to believe it over a period of time, choosing to ignore the seeress's words at first. But however she felt about the "curse" placed upon her, the fact is that Sarah Winchester moved West in 1884, after purchasing an eight-room farmhouse near San Jose, California, from a man known only as Dr. Caldwell.

After settling into the house, she hired a team of servants to cater to her needs, but, more significantly, she hired a staff of carpenters and ordered them to add a room onto the house. It was the first of the added rooms that would eventually make of this eight-room farmhouse a 160-room mystery house the real-life picture of what became one frightened woman's fears.

Sarah had apparently decided to take the seeress at her word, for she ordered the carpenters and workmen to organize themselves into shifts that would let the building go on round-the-clock: "Never stop building." And they did so, building rooms and additions at Sarah's behest and direction, although she knew nothing whatsoever about architecture or construction. What she did have was almost unlimited funds, no responsibilities, and an unreasoning dread of the future she might have if she stopped adding rooms to the ever-expanding house. Therefore each night she retired to the room only she could enter, called the séance room. In that room the spirits would tell her how to continue the work, and in the morning their instructions were passed on to the workmen on duty.

THAT'S INCREDIBLE!

The work was haphazard at best, but obviously—no doubt because the work was steady, on a lifetime basis for many of the builders—there were no complaints. Carpenters contentedly built one room onto the house only to hear from Mrs. Winchester that the room was to be torn down and rebuilt another way. By this process—building, tearing down, remodeling, rebuilding—Mrs. Winchester's extraordinary house shouldered its way to the sky, searching for more and more room on the 161-acre estate. Eventually the outbuildings surrounding the original eight-room farmhouse had to be torn down to accommodate the growing main house, which had come to be called, on formal occasions, Llanda Villa. The building reportedly cost one thousand dollars a day—in preinflation dollars—365 days a year, twenty-four hours a day.

But never mind the cost, thought Mrs. Winchester, with her bottomless pocketbook and no one to spend her money on. The rooms were added. Rooms built within rooms were constructed, and reconstructed. Eventually the house was seven storeys high, but as the process continued, it was again reduced to four storeys.

The eventual cost of Sarah's house has been estimated at approximately $5.5 million. Statistics inside the house boggle the mind: 10,000 windows, 47 fireplaces, 17 chimneys, 40 bedrooms, 52 skylights, 376 stairsteps on 40 staircases, 13 bathrooms, 467 doorways, 950 exit/entrance doors, 1,200 cabinet doors. The house was, needless to say, so complicated, so much like a live-in maze, that the servants—who numbered generally somewhere between eighteen and twenty—

THAT'S INCREDIBLE!

THAT'S INCREDIBLE!

were given floor plans and route guides to help them until they got used to the bizarre house. These floor plans, obviously, had to be changed constantly to reflect the changes Mrs. Winchester and her spirits had ordered in the house.

The spirits did not tell her everything directly, it seems. When something in Sarah's life displeased them, they left her "messages," and if she noticed them, she obeyed. There was, for instance, the matter of the wine cellar.

On one occasion, dining in her grand fashion with her secretary-companion, Mrs. Winchester went down to the wine cellar (which, because she could afford the best, contained only the finest of vintage wines), to which only she possessed a key. There was a special bottle she was looking for, but as she reached for it, she noticed a black hand print on the wall. The hand print was not hers, but whose else could it be? After all, she alone possessed a key to the cellar.

But that night, alone in the séance room, she asked about the print and was told it had been left by a demon's hand. To Sarah this was an obvious warning against alcohol, and the following morning she ordered the carpenters to wall the wine cellar up. They did a remarkable job, so thorough that the offending fine wines—which would now be as valuable as buried treasure to connoisseurs of such things—have never been found.

Whim—Sarah's and her spirits'—was everywhere in the house. There are miles and miles of winding, twisting, baffling corridors that lead to dead ends, as well as many secret passageways concealed in the walls themselves. The door of one passageway is the rear wall of an icebox.

THAT'S INCREDIBLE!

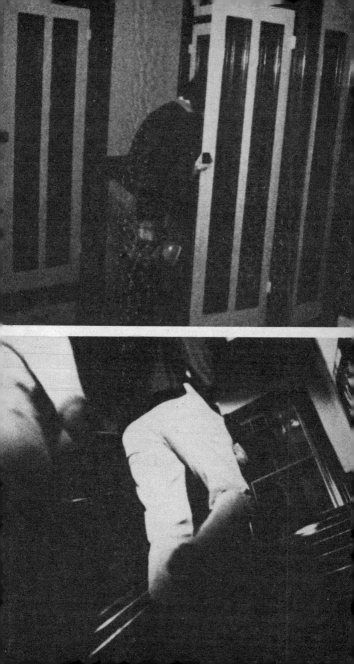

Many rooms have two doors—one of standard height, another designed for Mrs. Winchester's tiny, four-foot-ten-inch frame.

There is a stairway with seven turns and forty-four steps. It rises only nine feet. There is a spiral staircase with forty-three steps. Each step is only two inches high. There are other stairways that lead nowhere and melt into walls or even ceilings.

There is a linen closet as large as a three-room apartment. Not so strange, perhaps, in a house that must have required a lot of linens. But right next to it is a cupboard that is less than an inch deep.

There is a room that is filled with trapdoors.

There is a special window, priced at $10,000 at the turn of the century and probably priceless now, set into a wall by a stairway that connects two floors. Made of cut prisms, the window is designed to turn ordinary sunlight into multiple rainbows. But the window is set into a wall where no direct sunlight will ever fall.

Surely the placement of this extraordinary window was a mistake? Not absolutely, for Mrs. Winchester had her ways of dealing with mistakes. Her foreman, John Hansen—who, like the other workmen, never argued with her, no matter how strange her ideas—would listen to her directions and do as he was told. Sometimes her meanings were lost on him, as his executions of her directions would displease the eccentric lady. When that happened, there was what Mrs. Winchester considered a simple solution: the error might be sealed up, built over or around, or all of the preceding and then ripped out altogether.

No expense was spared. Mrs. Winchester spent

about a million dollars on antiques and artifacts such as Tiffany windows and priceless chandeliers. While many rooms went unfinished, some of those which were completed feature stained-glass doors and windows and similar elegant furnishings, brought from the corners of the world. Six warehouses full of uncrated furnishings were still to be unpacked in the mid-1930s.

Oddly no one was allowed to visit Mrs. Winchester in her home, with a very few exceptions. There were servants, teams of carpenters and workmen, but the curious who stopped to gawk at the house—which eventually covered six acres of the estate—had to be content with what they could see from a distance.

One particular hopeful visitor was turned away: President Theodore Roosevelt, who, in 1903, knocked at the door of the Winchester House. He hoped to tell the Winchester widow how much he appreciated the craftsmanship of the celebrated rifle, and certainly he would not have minded having a look inside the extraordinary house. But it was not to be. Even the venerable Teddy was refused admission to the mansion.

"My house is not open to strangers," the widow told him.

Thus he missed the baffling corridors, the road-to-nowhere staircases, the multiple fireplaces for ghosts who traveled in and out of the house through them, the recurring number thirteen, which Mrs. Winchester liked to use whenever possible: thirteen coathooks in closets, thirteen windows in a room, thirteen bathrooms, thirteen panels in a wall or ceiling, thirteen candles on a chandelier, thirteen steps in a staircase—the list is as apparently endless as the house itself seems to be.

The house was badly damaged in the earthquakes of 1906, and the workmen turned their attention to its repair. The work, and the additional building, continued as it had for years, until September 5, 1922. On that day the men left their work where it stood, and rows of unhammered nails can be seen where patient carpenters finally "finished" what for them had been an unending task. Its director, the old lady Sarah Winchester, who had employed hundreds of workmen to work round-the-clock for thirty-eight years, finally died

THAT'S INCREDIBLE!

at the age of eighty-three. Had the building kept her alive? Certainly there is no way to know. The seeress had never told her *when* the spirits would come for her—only that they would come.

But Sarah Winchester's death was by no means the end of the story of her endless mansion. The house was bought, almost immediately, by an outside interest, and the house was opened to visitors the following year. In 1925, Harry Houdini, the world-famous magician, toured the house at midnight, in hopes of dispelling belief in spiritualism for the house had already been labelled "haunted."

Even today, the home's caretaker, Brent Miller, tells stories of odd happenings around the house, where an aura of mystery lingers on. It was Miller himself who, as he made his nightly rounds of the many strange corridors, entered one particular room and—in the unearthly silence of such a vast, empty place—heard someone breathing. There was no one there.

On another occasion he heard footsteps and followed the sounds to the room in which Mrs. Winchester died. Again there was no one there. Miller later called the footsteps' bluff, calling them "No doubt just wind sounds." But many think there is a different answer.

In May, 1976, Antoinette May wrote in *Peninsula* magazine of spending a night in the Winchester House with members of the Nirvana Foundation, who intended to either authenticate or forever debunk the rumors that ghosts lurked in Mrs. Winchester's house.

Acting on frequent reports that various phenomena—chains rattling, whispers, footsteps—had been heard in the house, the Nirvana Foundation requested and received permission to spend the night in the house. There were five in the group: Nirvana Foundation cofounders Dal and Sylvia Brown, San Jose University photography department head Dick Schaskey, Nirvana research associate Ann Fockelman, and reporter Antoinette May. They came prepared with twelve opened packages of recording tape, a tape recorder, six cameras, and a metal detector.

Those who entered Sarah's séance room—off limits to every other human being during her lifetime—found a small blue room containing only a cabinet, armchair, table, paper, and a planchette board used for automatic writing. The Nirvana Foundation group made this their headquarters.

THAT'S INCREDIBLE!

Once they were settled, the house was closed for the night and everyone else left the premises until morning. The only exceptions were vicious attack dogs left outside to guard the grounds—so that once inside, no matter what happened, the group would have to remain inside the house until some-one arrived to remove the dogs.

Sylvia Brown—a psychic who had been careful *not* to look into the history, backgrounds, or lives of those involved with the house—heard organ music very soon after the group took up residence in the séance room. Her four companions did not hear the music, but definite organ sounds were picked up by the tape recorder. It is a known fact that Sarah Winchester possessed an organ and en-joyed playing it.

The entire group saw moving lights, for which there were no sources, and they also encountered unexplained cold spots. Later, sitting in Mrs. Winchester's bedroom, Sylvia and Antoinette saw large balls of red light that seemed to "explode" and then fade.

At one point Sylvia began to describe a couple, a man and woman, standing across the room and watching the group with fierce intensity. Dressed in clothing appropriate to Mrs. Winchester's time, Sylvia thought they might be the spirits of servants. Sarah's servants had been fiercely loyal, guarding her privacy jealously. Were they guarding her privacy against these strangers even now?

The eerie sense of being watched grew only greater as the night went on. Sylvia herself called the spirits she sensed in the Chinese drawing room, one of Sarah's favorites, "ominous." The group watched ghostly shadows flicker on the walls, and tried in vain to find a source from which light might be emanating. The atmosphere became more oppressive and terrifying, building and building to a point beyond which it was inconceivable the group could be more afraid.

Then, incredibly, Antoinette May said to herself, "I'm not afraid anymore. This is just an old house."

At the same moment Ann said, "I'm not afraid anymore. I don't think there's anyone here."

Sylvia said, "You're right. They've gone. They've all gone. We were surrounded by ugly, ominous shapes, but they've left us and gone away."

The night had begun as a terrifying ordeal; it ended with the Nirvana Foundation group laugh-

THAT'S INCREDIBLE!

ing together, drinking coffee they had ignored for hours, and wearily waiting for the caretaker to come and remove the dogs.

While the members of the Nirvana Foundation packed its gear from the house to their cars, the restoration procedures—slow but sure—at work in the house began for another day. The house has been undergoing major interior and exterior repair and restoration since 1973.

General manager Keith Kittle says that refurbishing projects have already required some 13,000 gallons of paint, hundreds of feet of handcrafted wooden rain gutters and ridgecresting, dozens of retooled wooden filials, and thousands of special shingles. Each of the many stained glass windows was taken out and realigned by Santa Cruz, California, craftsman Cecil Brussey.

And the restoration has not stopped at the house. A numer of old glass-plate photographs of the house and grounds were found in a shed and, working from these, conservators have put in thousands of plants in configurations like those found in the house's original, lush Victorian gardens. All the bushes and plants originally planted by Mrs. Winchester are being saved. Her fabulous fountains were painstakingly rebuilt, with a single new feature: recirculation pumps were installed in order to save water.

Even the glass in the greenhouse has been replaced. Flowers grown in the reconstructed building will be cut and used to brighten up the house.

The work is hard, but it pays off. In 1974, Sarah Winchester's incredible house was named a California Historical Landmark and placed on the National Register of Historic Places, where it certainly belongs.

Such designations provide prestige and recognition, however, and not money, something that the Winchester House and its restoration need a lot of to keep going. The house is a year-long attraction—open every day of the year except Christmas—to thousands of tourists. Whether the owners of the landmark, who call themselves Winchester Mystery House, Inc., have enough money to keep it open is, in itself, a mystery.

But for now, as guests from every part of the globe visit the wonderful, lavish Victorian puzzle in which Sarah Winchester lived, it is possible to understand that, even if the "spirits" Sarah so greatly feared did finally take her from the earthly world, her home—the world's largest and strangest dwelling—has achieved for her and for itself a kind

of eternal life.

When *That's Incredible's* crew visited the Winchester House, there was no resisting a small prank. Given a few minutes lead time, host John Davidson hid out in the world's best hide-and-seek house, pursued by a group of lucky lookers. They searched quite a while, falling prey to many of Sarah Winchester's architectural tricks, before finally finding John in the séance room.